The Historic
Country Hotels of France

A Select Guide

WENDY ARNOLD

The Historic
Country Hotels of France

A Select Guide

Photographs by
ROBIN MORRISON

CHRONICLE BOOKS

SAN FRANCISCO

For Norbert and Jean Bosquillon de Frescheville
and their family

Frontispiece: Michel Troisgros (left) with his fellow chefs in the kitchens at Troisgros.

Opposite: Dinner is laid at Pic, Jacques Pic's celebrated restaurant in Valence.

First published in the United States 1988 by Chronicle Books.

Printed in Spain by Edime/Graphiberia, S. A.
D. L. M.: 21383-1988

Library of Congress Cataloging in Publication Data

Arnold, Wendy.
    The historic country hotels of France: a select guide/Wendy Arnold; photographs by Robin Morrison.
        p. cm.
    Includes index.
    ISBN 0-87701-545-7
    1. Hotels, taverns, etc.—France—Guide-books. 2. France–
–Description and travel—1975– —Guide-books.   I. Morrison, Robin, 1944– .   II. Title.
    TX910.F8A76 1988
    647'.9444—dc 19

88-11728
CIP

Distributed in Canada by
Raincoast Books,
112 East Third Avenue,
Vancouver, B.C. V5T 1C8

10 9 8 7 6 5 4 3 2 1

Chronicle Books
San Francisco, California

Contents

Preface

A romantic evening view of the dining room at Le Vieux Logis, Trémolat. See p. 69.

Especially memorable for the gourmet, but unforgettable even for the most experienced world traveler, are the historic hotels scattered throughout the glorious countryside of France. Turreted châteaux, mirrored in the smooth water of their moats; ancient stone water-mills beside mountain streams; stately mansions furnished with priceless antiques; sturdy farmhouses owned by the same family for four hundred years; craggy mountain fastnesses looking out over the blue Mediterranean: all have become welcoming, comfortable, and elegant hotels.

I first visited France nearly forty years ago and have returned many times since. I was therefore delighted that when my books on the historic hotels of London and the English countryside proved popular, I was asked to write about similar hotels throughout France. Driving many thousands of kilometers, I rediscovered the excellence of its roads, the charm of its many different landscapes – mountains, forests, lakes, vineyards, and beaches – and the fascination of its ancient towns, soaring Gothic cathedrals, stormy headlands, and picturesque medieval villages. I passed many happy hours discussing with chefs the specialities of their region's cuisine and the merits of its wines and cheeses.

Yet, as in England I found that many famous hotels with equally high ratings varied dramatically – some were delightful and some were disappointing. At the very least I expected the hotels to be as comfortable as my own home – why pay to stay anywhere, no matter how picturesque, if one is going to suffer? They had to be scrupulously clean, with good bathrooms (preferably with showers), comfortable beds – not old and sagging – excellent food, and a friendly and efficient welcome. Thirty years backing-up my husband's business career, living all over the world, running large households and entertaining rulers and diplomats gave me a sharp eye for a dusty corner or smeary teaspoon. Where possible I visited them alone, since their attitude toward a middle-aged lady traveling unaccompanied was a good test of the welcome they offered. I arrived incognita, did not tell owners what I was doing until after paying the bill, and did not accept any hospitality or fee for inclusion in the book.

Many of the famous hotels of the French countryside were once country inns, run by villagers who cooked simple but sublime meals from local fresh ingredients. Their descendants have continued the family tradition, but, trained in Paris or a big-town establishment, they have often returned to create sophisticated menus, transforming a simple inn into a sumptuously luxurious hotel and winning Michelin's coveted three-star rating in the process. Their well-trained staff keeps standards high, fashionable people are seen at their tables, and guests have the pleasure of meeting their host when he emerges from the kitchen, dressed in immaculate white, to enjoy his well-deserved applause. This is not to everybody's taste, so for those who would prefer owners to stay in their kitchens and attend solely to the running of their hotels, I have tracked down several less worldly establishments. Their style is simpler, the decor less opulent and the menu is more likely to reflect local traditions. Some may prefer the formal period splendor of the châteaux, with their attentive staff and splendid antique furniture; others will enjoy the rustic peace of a simple country inn. The aim of this book is to help the reader to make an informed choice of hotel, of whatever character, where the prices charged will be fairly matched by the level of comfort provided.

This is a personal selection of some of my favorite hotels in my favorite regions of France. They are all very different, but each one is an attractive historic building in a beautiful area of France well worth visiting and exploring. English is spoken in all the hotels, and owners or managers will be delighted to tell guests what there is to see locally. All serve delicious food, including regional specialities, and all have helpful and courteous staff. These are hotels to which I would return with immense pleasure, and to which I would with confidence send even the most demanding of my friends.

General Information

Preparation The peak travel months in France are July and August (worst dates to travel: 14 July, 1 and 30 August, second week in September). A pleasant time to tour is May and June, and from mid-September to the end of October, just after many hotels have opened for the year, or just before they close for winter. In these months, prices are usually lower, roads less crowded, hotels less full, and there is the added bonus of spring blossoms, or autumnal colors and wine festivals. European weather being unpredictable, it is useful to travel with light clothing that can be built up in layers, at least one really warm outfit, and a raincoat. Dress in more expensive luxury hotels, and especially in those with three Michelin gourmet stars, tends towards formality; jackets and ties and dresses are expected in the evening, even in the countryside.

Hotels should always be booked well in advance, and you should detail any wishes for a special diet, a six-foot bed, an extra-firm mattress, a large room with space for much baggage, a wall-mounted shower, access without stairs, a suite, a view, or a room of equivalent comfort to that of others traveling with you. Since the hotels I have chosen have been created from existing houses rather than being custom-built, the above features may not be provided automatically. Please note that many hotels in France close entirely for one day each week and for several months in winter or summer. This adds considerable challenge and interest to planning an itinerary! The motel chain Novotel has sites on main highways and on the edge of large towns, and can be useful for filling in geographic gaps (tel: in the USA, 212 752 7430; in the UK, 01 752 2140).

Non-French-speakers should ideally take a phrasebook. Somebody who speaks English is available in all the hotels in the book, but this is not necessarily the case in shops or small restaurants.

Terms Since prices can fluctuate, I have given only rough guidelines. I have divided the hotels into three broad categories based on what they charge for dinner for two (excluding wine unless specified) and a standard double room for one night. Government taxes, cover charges, and service are included, although some hotels quote them separately. The approximate dollar and sterling equivalents are based on a rate of 10FF = $1.80 or £1.00.

Moderate	800–1299FF	(£80–129/$144–233)
Expensive	1300–1799FF	(£130–179/$234–322)
Deluxe	1800–2450FF	(£180–245/$323–441)

This does not include breakfast (charged separately), *à la carte* prices, drinks, phone calls, or other extras. Many hotels offer luxurious suites, but often at double standard room prices. Special seasonal bargains and 'demi-pension' rates, which include dinner and breakfast but not lunch, are sometimes available for longer stays; there may also be special reductions for families. Enquire when booking.

Getting there I have added the approximate distances of the hotels by road from Paris. The main autoroutes are excellent, with speed limits marked in kilometers per hour, but usually charge quite an expensive toll. Alternative free, fast routes via side roads are marked on road signs and on maps with green arrows. Other side roads can be narrow and winding, and are very slow through towns. Traffic coming from the right always has priority, unless road signs indicate otherwise.

Some airlines provide fly/drive packages, and there is an excellent network of internal flights, as well as trains and buses. French Government Tourist Offices in most capital cities provide copious, helpful information and concessionary tickets.

Eating in France Each region has its own local cooking, wines, and cheeses which are well worth exploring. Most owners try to include regional dishes on their menus, and will suggest appropriate local wines. There is often a local fruit brandy for after dinner. Most hotels provide both a simple and an elaborate set menu; either is usually better value than eating *à la carte*. You should enquire whether tax and service are included. If you ask for a cup of coffee, it will usually arrive small, strong, and black, except at breakfast, when it appears in an outsize cup with lots of hot milk; you should specify your wishes. The French usually drink mineral water at table, ordered by the bottle, of which the still Evian and fizzy Perrier are perhaps the best known. Be sure to book your table for dinner when you book your accommodation, to avoid disappointment. Should you simply want a sandwich in your room, it is worth checking on prices to avoid a shock. You may experience difficulty requesting simplified dishes in any of the hotels in this book, since the chefs are the nation's superstar artists and may have spent years perfecting a particular sauce. I would, however, expect the staff in all these hotels to behave with perfect courtesy at all times, and I should be most grateful to hear (via my publishers) of any difficulties.

An alphabetical index of hotels and their locations appears on page 96.

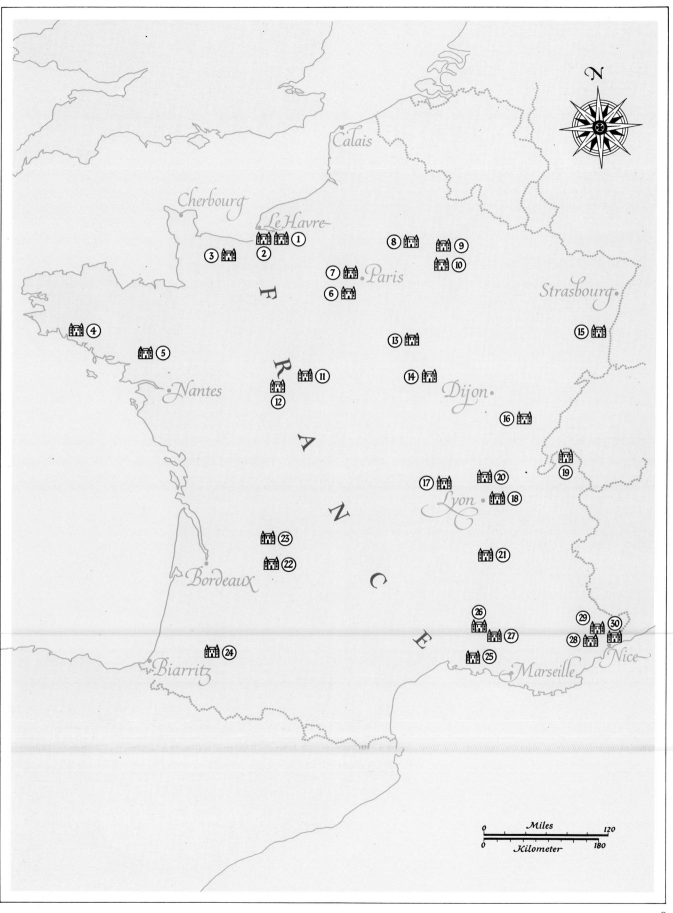

N

Calais

Cherbourg

Le Havre
① ②
③

⑧ ⑨
⑩
⑦
Paris
⑥

Strasbourg

④
⑤

⑬

⑮

F
R
A
N
C
E

⑪
⑫

⑭
Dijon

⑯

Nantes

⑰
⑲
⑳
⑱
Lyon

㉓
㉒

㉑

Bordeaux

㉖
㉗
㉙ ㉚
㉘
Nice
㉔
㉕
Marseille

Biarritz

Miles
0   120
0   180
Kilometer

9

A traditional Normandy inn

The Auberge du Vieux Puits is a charming 17th-century inn, beamed inside and out, built around a courtyard filled with flowers and a huge willow tree. The cobbled entrance hallway leads to rooms with stone-flagged floors, low ceilings, and tiny mullioned windows bright with red-checked gingham curtains. This is the perfect setting for a fascinating collection of local antiques, lovingly assembled over the years by the owners, Jacques Foltz, son of an artist and himself no mean painter, and his wife, Hélène. A warmly welcoming couple (both speak excellent English), they have successfully preserved the atmosphere of this traditional village inn, where local people mingle with travelers in the two small parlors. In each is an immense open hearth with a roaring log fire, and small wooden tables at which the proprietor serves guests the superb food (Michelin-starred, Gault-Millau-laurel wreathed), cooked by two young chefs under his close supervision.

Their ancient well is described by Gustave Flaubert in *Madame Bovary*, hence the 'Trout Bovary' in champagne sauce with which I began my dinner; the delicious fish had been freshly caught in a local brook. A sorbet made from young Calvados cleared the palate for duckling, casserolled with sharp morello cherries and herbs. A local farmhouse camembert was at the exact moment of ideal ripeness; the inn's own special pear tart with a hint of apricot was served with thick Normandy cream, and splendid coffee and sweetmeats concluded a marvellous meal. There is an excellent cellar with a good range of reasonably priced wines.

All the bedrooms at the inn look out on to the quiet courtyard. My small but comfortable room was in a new building, constructed in traditional Normandy style but with modern bathrooms, plentiful hanging space, central heating, new beds, color TV, and phones. It had blue flowered curtains, plain country-style wooden furniture, and was spotlessly clean. For the purist connoisseur, Madame Foltz has preserved the old bedrooms in the original 17th-century building in all their unmodernized charm, with sloping floors, beamed ceilings and antique beds, but opens them only from March to November.

I fell in love with the Auberge du Vieux Puits from the moment I received their letter replying to my request for accommodation. I was offered a room "in our recent wing, located in the garden, in a quiet situation." The letter continued: "Considering the modest size of our rooms, as well as the richness of our food, we do not really recommend longlasting stays." I felt that such ungrasping people must be delightful, and so they proved to be.

The Auberge is at the heart of a picturesque village, full of interesting little shops and boutiques, and conveniently close to several of the Channel ports. This is the sort of simple and charming inn one always searches for and so rarely finds.

A glimpse of the courtyard at this rustic inn (opposite), whose specialities are good food and fine Calvados. The interiors, furnished with antiques (above) are both snug and elegant (overleaf, right, one of the upstairs sitting rooms).

AUBERGE DU VIEUX PUITS, 6 rue Notre-Dame-du-Pré, 27500 Pont-Audemer. **Tel.** 32 41 01 48. **Telex** None. **Owners** Jacques and Hélène Foltz. **Closed** 20 Dec.–22 Jan.; 27 June–first week in July, and every Monday evening and Tuesday (all day). **Rooms** 12 double, 6 with bathroom (incl. shower), direct-dial phone, TV. **Facilities** 2 sitting rooms (open Mar.–Nov. only), 3 dining rooms, courtyard with parking. **Restrictions** Dogs in bedrooms only. **Terms** Moderate. **Credit cards** Visa. **Getting there** From Paris, A 13, exit Pont-Audemer. Signposts in village. 168 km. **Of local interest** Normandy Landing beaches; Bayeux Tapestry; Honfleur. **Whole day expeditions** Rouen; Romanesque abbeys of Jumièges and St Wandrille; Monet's house at Giverny; Abbaye du Bec Hellouin. **Lunching out** Pavé d'Auge, Beuvron-en-Auge; Auberge Vieux Logis, Conteville; St-Pierre, La Bouille; Bertrand Warin, Beffroy, Gill, Rouen.

Atelier of the Impressionists

Should you wish to sleep in what was once the *atelier* of a famous Impressionist painter and is now a comfortable, elegantly-furnished hotel room, you will enjoy a visit to La Ferme Saint-Siméon. Eugène Boudin and his pupil Claude Monet, Corot, Courbet, Sisley, Dufy and many others came here to paint, and to enjoy the excellent cooking of La Mère Toutain in what was then a simple thatched Normandy farmhouse, and is today a sophisticated country hotel. Then as now, guests were drawn to Saint-Siméon by its views across the tranquil estuary of the river Seine. They would stroll down to the tiny historic port of Honfleur, whose wooden church was built by shipwrights celebrating the final withdrawal of the English at the end of the Hundred Years War in the mid-15th century, and from where in the 1660s small boats sailed off across the Atlantic to people a new colony in Quebec with Normans. They also made expeditions further afield, to the bustling town of Trouville, or to Deauville with its boardwalk and racetrack. Whatever they saw inspired them to paint – sometimes even sitting under the apple trees at La Ferme Saint-Siméon.

Today's visitor who does not wish to climb the stairs to the artists' rooms, or who finds the excellent modern bathrooms fitted into the 17th-century structure too small, may walk a few yards to Le Pressoir. This new building, named for the farm's cider press, has a traditional appearance, but inside there is an elevator to whisk guests up to large custom-built bedrooms furnished with tasteful designer fabrics, a blend of antique and modern furniture and vast marble bathrooms. A manor house with its own grounds and tennis court a few hundred yards down the road offers traditional grandeur as a third choice.

The present owners of La Ferme Saint-Siméon, the Boelen family, returning to Normandy roots after eleven years of running a mountain hotel, have preserved the personality of their new empire with care and taste. They sought out massive ancient oak beams from demolished local farmhouses for the ceiling when enlarging the restaurant and have maintained the building's traditional link with painters by setting aside an upper gallery for local artists to exhibit their work for sale. One of the sons supervises the kitchen; his English-born wife assists English-speaking visitors. The local fishing fleet guarantees a plentiful supply of excellent seafood for the varied and appetizing menu.

Arriving one winter afternoon I was warmly greeted in the beamed hallway, where there was a discreet, well-stocked boutique. I later enjoyed dinner in front of an enormous fire in the stone fireplace, and had a most comfortable night in one of the centrally-heated modern bedrooms. Though the manor is shut in winter, the rest of this well-run hotel remains open. Just an hour by road from Le Havre, it provides a memorable first or last night in France for the comfort-seeking traveller.

A traditional cider press (above) has become a feature of the hotel's garden. The gracious building (opposite) contains charming, summery bedrooms.

LA FERME SAINT-SIMÉON ET SON MANOIR, rue Adolphe-Marais, 14600 Honfleur. **Tel.** 31 89 23 61. **Telex** 171 031 F. **Owners** The Boelen family. **Open** All year. **Rooms** 38 (incl. 5 suites), all with bathrooms (some with wall showers), direct-dial phone, and TV. **Facilities** 2 dining rooms, terrace, gardens, heated indoor pool, elevator (in Le Pressoir only), tennis court, helicopter landing, sea views. **Restrictions** None. **Terms** Expensive. **Credit cards** Access, Visa. **Getting there** From Paris, A 13, off at Deauville/Pont l'Evêque/Honfleur turning, D 579 through Honfleur to harbor, follow sea road W, turn L for hotel at lighthouse. 200 km. **Of local interest** Honfleur; Calvados distilleries; Normandy Landing beaches; Bayeux Tapestry. **Whole day expeditions** Rouen; Monet's house at Giverny; Romanesque abbeys of Jumièges and St Wandrille; Mont St Michel. **Lunching out** Auberge du Vieux Puits, Pont Audemer (see p. 11); Pavé d'Auge, Beuvron-en-Auge; Auberge Vieux Logis, Conteville.

3 Château d'Audrieu

Ancestral grandeur

The Château d'Audrieu and its lands were the ancestral domain of the Percy family, who crossed to England with William the Conqueror, and stayed to become Dukes of Northumberland. Among their direct descendants are the Livry-Level family who own and live in the château today.

Traces of the original moated stronghold remain in the beautifully landscaped grounds of the graceful 18th-century château, whose two wings of pale gray Caen stone form an open E enclosing a wide gravelled courtyard. Trapped between warring armies during the Normandy landings, it miraculously survived, and bears no visible scars. The entrance is at the side, not through the wrought-iron main gates, but near the walled flower and vegetable gardens. Madame Livry-Level welcomes guests in the small side entrance hall where an open fire burns cheerfully. From this lead a sitting room and excellently stocked bar, memorable for its local aged calvados. The bedrooms in this, the stable wing, are modestly sized. There are far grander, though naturally more expensive, bedrooms in the main body of the château and in the former family apartments in the north wing. Getting to these involves walking down long corridors that become progressively more splendid, furnished with antiques and hung with family portraits.

My huge, newly decorated, close-carpeted attic room had hand-hewn rafters, a magnificent marble bathroom, and blended fine antique and modern furniture in a tasteful decor of warm earth tones with touches of clear blues and golds.

Monsieur Livry-Level awaits his guests in the restaurant, seats them, and advises on wines. There are some outstanding burgundies and champagnes in a well-chosen and sensibly priced wine list. Under the low, white-painted beamed ceiling, silver gleams on starched napery in the firelight, among candles and fresh flowers. Above is a splendidly formal drawing room. The meal, fully justifying its Michelin star, was imaginative, delicate and delicious. I began with a langoustine consommé flavored with a touch of fresh ginger and progressed to superb sea bass with a masterly sweet-sour onion garnish and excellent vegetables. The final course, a fresh strawberry tart, was meltingly light. Breakfast was of like quality: an assortment of freshly-baked breads and croissants served on crested china, with coffee in a silver pot.

Sometimes organizations or companies take over the whole château, and the owners then recreate "la vie du château," a house party with ballooning, horse-drawn carriage rides, shooting, and hunting, for which green-jacketed huntsmen assemble in the courtyard, sounding their traditional twirly French horns. Sometimes world-renowned politicians and their retinues come to relax in this setting of gracious tranquility.

All guests, however, receive the same friendly welcome, excellent service and warm hospitality that has been the tradition of the Livry-Level family for more than nine centuries.

This stately château's elegant rooms (opposite) are a fit setting for the Michelin-starred food (above).

CHÂTEAU D'AUDRIEU, 14250 Audrieu par Tilly-sur-Seulles. **Tel.** 31 80 21 52 (3 lines). **Telex** 171 777F. **Owner** Gérard Livry-Level. **Closed** 20 Dec.–20 Jan. and open only for private groups, conferences, etc., 1 Dec.–19 Dec. and 21 Jan.–1 Mar. Closed all Wed. and Thurs. lunch. **Rooms** 28 (incl. 4 suites), all with bathroom (10 with wall shower), direct-dial phone, 5 with TV (available in other bedrooms by request), 8 on ground floor. **Facilities** Drawing room, sitting room, bar, restaurant, heated pool, walled park-lands, helicopter landing, tennis nearby. **Restrictions** No dogs in restaurant. **Terms** Expensive. **Credit cards** Access, Visa. **Getting there** From Paris, A13 to Caen, N13 (towards Bayeux) 12 km, L on D158 dir. Tilly-sur-Seulles, château on L. 240 km. **Of local interest** Bayeux Tapestry; Normandy Landing beaches; Caen's Romanesque churches. **Whole day expeditions** Mont St Michel (crowded in summer). **Lunching out** La Bourride, Caen; Manoir d'Hastings, Benouville.

Beside a mill stream

This intriguing hotel is come upon unexpectedly. After passing through an unremarkable little seaside town, the road enters the leafy valley of the river Belun, famous for its oysters, trout, and salmon. The turning to the hotel leads steeply down to reveal a wide lake surrounded by a cluster of 16th-century buildings, and thronged with wildfowl. Mills, barns, storehouses and byres are dotted about between colorful flower beds, overhanging trees, fast-rushing millstreams, and the river itself. Once the mills of the Dukes of Burgundy, these buildings have now become a unique and delightful hotel.

The main entrance to the hotel opens into a tiny hallway, then into a high room lined with pine, where there is a long bar and a view of an enormous working water wheel. From here solid ancient stairways lead past the original massive mill machinery into the restaurant, a series of low, stone-flagged rooms overlooking the river. The bedrooms are spread throughout the many scattered buildings. Some are fairly simple, others occupy entire tiny houses, which retain their original cogged mill gears and heavy oak beams. In some the bed is tucked away on a gallery and comfortable chairs are arranged snugly in front of a log fire blazing on a raised stone hearth. Carpets, telephones, modern bathrooms, and minibars are fitted in harmoniously, so that many of the charms of camping or staying in a mountain chalet are combined with the comforts of a hotel. A track links the buildings, so that in wet weather guests can drive from their bedroom to the dining rooms, while in sunny weather they have only to walk up to the hotel, following the course of the millstreams.

The Quistrebert family have owned one mill since 1968, and later bought another nearby, while gradually restoring and converting the buildings. They have secured the services of an excellent chef, Xavier Gabard, who uses fresh local produce and seafood with skill and imagination in his elegantly presented food. There is much to do at the hotel, with a heated indoor pool, fishing in the river or sea, and hunting further up the valley.

This is the perfect base for exploring Brittany, whose well-named Côte Sauvage has wildly beautiful and turbulent seas breaking over jagged rocks. There are picturesque ancient fishing ports, and the yet more ancient – and eerie – avenues of huge prehistoric stones standing amid heather and wild flowers. Also worth visiting are the artists' colonies, studios selling painted pottery, the bay of Morbihan with many tiny islands, and the ancient city of Vannes. (Summer visitors should note, however, that the Brittany coast gets crowded during school holidays.)

I enjoyed the riverside woodland setting of this hotel, and its relaxed atmosphere, and admired the enterprise of the family who have restored these historic buildings so imaginatively and given them new life.

The view over the river from the dining room windows (opposite) makes the experience of Xavier Gabard's food (above, a lobster dish) all the more memorable. Overleaf: the front of the hotel, facing a plough, lake, and ducks.

LES MOULINS DU DUC, 29116 Moëlan-sur-Mer. **Tel.** 98 39 60 73. **Telex** 940 080F. **Owner** Robert Quistrebert. **Closed** Mid Jan. to early Mar., and every Wed. out of season. **Rooms** 27 (incl. 5 suites), all with bathroom (4 incl. shower), direct-dial phone, most with minibar, 15 with color TV. **Facilities** Sitting room with bar, restaurant, gardens with river, streams and lakes, heated indoor pool, helicopter landing, river and sea fishing, shooting. Tennis 2 km. **Restrictions** Dogs in bedrooms only. **Terms** Moderate. **Credit cards** All major cards. **Getting there** From Paris, A10/A11 (N23 if road not completed) to Nantes, N165, exit for Quimperlé. Into Quimperlé, out on D14 for Moëlan, hotel signposted there. 514 km. **Of local interest** Concarneau and other fishing ports; Gulf of Bénodet. **Whole day expeditions** Quimper (potteries); Côte Sauvage; Carnac prehistoric standing stones; Gulf of Morbihan. **Lunching out** Le Galion, Concarneau; La Taupinière, Moulin de Rosmadec, Pont Aven.

A gastronomic discovery

La Roche Bernard has a yacht harbor and some attractive medieval houses. The main road that follows the Brittany coast passes beside the town, rather than going through, making it a convenient, quiet stopping place for the traveler. The Auberge Bretonne, an old house which was once a traditional *crêperie*, or pancake house, is not in one of the little town's more picturesque streets, but it would be wrong to dismiss it for lack of outward show.

Open the door of the Auberge and you will find the main restaurant on your right, a small dining room also to your right, and the steep stairs which lead up to the bedrooms immediately in front of you. The stiffly starched tablecloths, the shining silverware, and the welcoming smile of Solange Thorel, slim, blonde and efficient, tell you that the owners are people who care. This is very much a restaurant with rooms, not an elaborate hotel. Visitors come for the food, and the few simple but tasteful and spotlessly clean bedrooms, with shining tiled bathrooms, have been provided for guests planning on more than a day's journey. Furnished with pleasant country antiques and pretty fabrics, the rooms vary in size but all have central heating, fitted carpets, good reading lights and ample hanging space.

Jacques Thorel, young, serious, dedicated, and with an impressive moustache, has trained with some of France's top chefs. He is said to have the finest cellar of wines in Brittany. In the gleaming new kitchens – of which he is justly proud – he produces inspired, imaginative, well-presented food, offered in a series of set menus to match every pocket.

I had decided to dine lightly, but looking through the choice of menus was seduced by the most elaborate, which began with delicious sea urchins stuffed with scallops and endive, in a delicate pink sauce. A light lobster pancake, mildly flavored with fresh ginger and served with tender salsify, was followed by sea bass, garnished with spices and arranged on a bed of slightly caramelized sliced baby carrots. Then came a traditional local harvesters' dish: young rabbit cooked with foie gras, wrapped in a cabbage leaf, and accompanied by chanterelles (wild wood-mushrooms). To finish, there was delicious local cheese and *les delices de Solange*, an assortment of small deserts – one chocolate, one creamy (in the shape of a heart), and one a small tartlet of wild strawberries.

Many of France's most famous chefs have begun their careers in a small restaurant just like this. By dint of its owners' unflagging hard work and dedication, the Auberge Bretonne will undoubtedly gain stars and fame. Solange Thorel was as friendly and attentive when serving the breakfast coffee as she had been when pouring the final after-dinner brandy the night before; she makes guests staying in the hotel comfortable and welcome. The quality of Jacques Thorel's food easily equalled or excelled that of many of the starred establishments I visited, and the meal was excellent value for money. He keeps a range of menus at prices that allow local people to eat regularly at the Auberge, rather than transform his hotel and his prices into a luxury class affordable only by wealthy tourists. Not a place for seekers after lavish comforts, but definitely a goal for gourmets.

An excellent breakfast is laid on the garden terrace (opposite, above); in the sunny dining room guests enjoy Jacques Thorel's remarkable cooking and good cellars (above).

AUBERGE BRETONNE, 2 place du Guesclin, 56130 La Roche-Bernard. **Tel.** 99 90 60 28. **Telex** None. **Owners** Jacques and Solange Thorel. **Closed** 15 Nov.–15 Dec., all day Thurs., and Fri. lunch. **Rooms** 6, 5 with bathroom and direct-dial phone, 3 with color TV **Facilities** Restaurant, 2 other private dining rooms, small garden, tennis, golf, sea nearby. **Restrictions** None. **Terms** Moderate. **Credit cards** All major. **Getting there** From Paris A10/A11 Nantes, N165 to La Roche-Bernard, 2nd turning on L before the bridge, hotel on L in small square. 400 km. **Of local interest** Bay of Morbihan; national park at Brière. **Whole day expeditions** Carnac prehistoric standing stones; Nantes. **Lunching out** Castel Marie-Louise, L'Hermitage, La Baule; Delphin, Bellevue; Les Maraîchers, Nantes.

A ducal retreat

Like an illustration from a medieval Book of Hours, the pointed turrets of the Château d'Esclimont rise above the surrounding trees, and are mirrored in the still green waters of its encircling moat, upon which wild mallards fuss broods of ducklings, and pristine swans drift in elegantly indolent lethargy. A long drive leads through acres of landscaped parkland and over a river, to where a vista of the château suddenly opens up, a fairy-tale castle lost in the woods. Built in 1543, it has belonged to several ducal families. The last, the de La Rochefoucauld-Doudeauville, removed one of the four corner towers, thus opening the inner courtyard to the light and air, and engraved over the entrance door the family motto, "C'est mon plaisir": "This is my pleasure."

Today, in less than an hour by autoroute from Paris, one reaches the quiet little villages and peaceful countryside which still surround the château; the most hurried arrive by helicopter. Entering the hallway, visitors are greeted with as efficient and well-groomed a staff as one would hope to find in a Paris hotel. There are elevators up to the rooms, which vary from enormous apartments with hugely high ceilings, to a small round room with a round bed in one of the turrets. Their walls are lined with fine fabrics, bathrooms are modern and marble, and there are further suites in a hunting pavilion on the far side of the moat. Rooms are snugly warm in winter, cool in summer. Mine overlooked the moat and the wooded hillside beyond. The tall window's wooden shutters were closed for me at night. An enormous black marble fireplace dominated the room, which had a glittering chandelier, wooden panelling, and a wide bed with a cover that matched the chintz of the armchairs.

The four dining rooms, one lined with fine gilded leather, all with beautiful views, have white damask cloths, gleaming silverware, fresh flowers on the tables, and an appealing menu. A brisk walk in the grounds had sharpened my appetite for an excellent bisque and hare in a rich red-wine sauce with fresh pasta, followed by tasty regional cheese, featherlight pancakes served with fresh orange sorbet, and delicate petits fours. Presentation of the food is delightful, portions are generous; Gault-Millau awards two toques.

For the summer visitor, there is a tennis court and heated swimming pool as well as innumerable pleasant woodland paths for walking or jogging. During the winter months, concerts are arranged in the vast Trophy Room. The château is one of several magnificent historic treasures rescued from a ruinous state by René Traversac, transformed into splendid hotels, and given back the life and grandeur they once possessed, under the watchful eye of dedicated and highly professional managers. At the Château d'Esclimont one may enjoy the efficiency of a town hotel in the glorious setting of a ducal country retreat.

Glimpses of the château's splendid interiors are shown opposite: flowers in the dining room, a marble bathroom and (below) a bedroom. Above and overleaf: the peaceful grounds include a stretch of river.

CHÂTEAU D'ESCLIMONT, Saint-Symphorien-le-Château, 28700 Auneau. **Tel.** 37 31 15 15. **Telex** 780 560. **Owners** Grandes Etapes Françaises (René Traversac). **Managers** Raymond and Nicole Spitz. **Open** All year. **Rooms** 54 double (incl. 6 suites), all with bathrooms (most with hand showers, 2 with wall showers), direct-dial phone, color TV, minibar. **Facilities** 4 dining rooms, bar, 3 drawing rooms, elevators, helicopter landing, extensive parkland and gardens, 2 tennis courts, heated pool, boating. Hot-air ballooning by arrangement. **Restrictions** No dogs in public rooms. **Terms** Expensive. **Credit card** Visa. **Getting there** A10 from Paris, 65 km, about 1 hour. 6 km w of Ablis on N10, direction Chartres. Orly airport 45 km. **Of local interest** Versailles, Chartres. **Whole day expeditions** Palace of Fontainebleau, Loire Valley and its châteaux, Monet's house at Giverny. **Lunching out** Host. Blanche de Castille, Dourdan; Les Hauts de Port Royal, St-Lambert.

28

7 Cazaudehore et La Forestière
Saint-Germain-en-Laye, Ile de France

In the woods near Paris

Louis XIV was baptized in the château of Saint-Germain-en-Laye and later lived there while his palace at Versailles was being built. No doubt he often hunted in the royal forests which to this day surround the château. Shortly after World War I, Monsieur Cazaudehore set up a small refreshment stand in the heart of the forest at the gates of the local military establishment. Badly gassed at Verdun, his health required an open-air life, and his career as a *maître d'hôtel* had proved too strenuous. After some years, with the help of his family, the stand became a small restaurant, and eventually a famous, Michelin-starred establishment, which features specialities of Béarn, from where the family originally came. The ancient high Pyrenean lands of Béarn in the south-west were known to the Romans and were passed through by pilgrims to Santiago de Compostela, as well as being the birthplace of France's King Henry of Navarre.

More recently La Forestière, a hotel with comfortable, elegant bedrooms and a sitting room, has been built in the garden of the restaurant. It is run by the third generation of Cazaudehores, though all three generations still work together in both hotel and restaurant, ensuring unflagging standards.

This is a most delightful spot. Near a town only twenty minutes by métro from the heart of Paris, the restaurant is charming and sophisticated in a rustic style. There is a covered terrace for winter, and in summer tables are set out on the grass among the bright flowerbeds. I enjoyed an excellent meal from an interesting menu – a light bavarois of vegetables, with a hint of basil, perfect roast lamb fragrant with rosemary, and a mouth-watering plate of *gourmandises*, small assorted desserts. Everything was impeccably served on tables with crisp pink cloths, fresh flowers, and pretty candlesticks.

Strolling across the garden after dinner, I noticed that the handle on the glass door of La Forestière was an old weaving shuttle, and that the stairs were decorated with the carved wooden blocks used for hand-printing fabrics with elaborate designs. My small top-floor suite was furnished with an antique carved bed, 18th-century prints, and brass reading lamps. The walls were lined with a pretty greeny-blue patterned cloth. A modern bathroom and deep hanging closet with minibar linked the bedroom to the small sitting room furnished with comfortable modern armchairs, from which I looked straight out into the branches of an oak tree. Breakfasting next morning in my room I watched a squirrel leaping from branch to branch, and a tree-creeper busily foraging upside down for insects in the oak's rough bark.

There are tennis courts next door, riding in the forest, and golf nearby. Versailles is only a few miles away: if you wish, a local driver will take you there, or into Paris, which is close enough to explore by day before returning to the leafy quiet of La Forestière for the night.

The woods come up to the hotel windows (above); inside are elegant bedrooms (opposite, top right). The fortunate guests can dine outside in summer; the night-time view shows the restaurant from the garden.

CAZAUDEHORE ET LA FORESTIÈRE, 1 avenue du Président Kennedy, 78100 Saint-Germain-en-Laye, Ile de France. **Tel** (1) 3 451 93 80/39 73 36 60. **Telex** 696 055F. **Owners** Cazaudehore family. **Closed** Restaurant only closes on Mon., except for public holidays. **Rooms** 30 (incl. 6 suites) all with bathroom (incl. wall shower), radio, direct-dial phone, color TV. **Facilities** Restaurant, bar. In hotel, sitting room, elevator. Gardens, forest, tennis next door, riding/golf nearby. **Restrictions** None. **Terms** Expensive. **Credit cards** Access, Visa. **Getting there** From Paris N13/N190/N186/N184 dir. Pontoise, turning to hotel on L, hotel at end on L. Métro station (Saint-Germain) 1½ km away. **Of local interest** Château of Saint-Germain; Versailles; Napoleon's house, Malmaison. **Whole day expeditions** Monet's house at Giverny; Musée Condé, Chantilly; Paris. **Lunching out** Trois Marches, Versailles; Le Tastevin, Maisons-Lafitte; ask hotel about Paris restaurants.

A magnificent mansion

The impressive ruins of a 13th-century château stand on a rocky outcrop surrounded by what is more a chasm than a moat, amid the green wooded countryside of Picardy. On the site of the château's lower courtyard, between outer wall and moat, is a magnificent 16th-century Renaissance mansion, with a tall tower and one of the original round gray-stone wall-turrets built into its structure. This is the Hostellerie du Château.

Two generations of the Blot family came to the Hostellerie in 1956, and between them still look after every aspect of their guests' comfort, from reception desk and decor, to restaurant and kitchens. The mansion stands in trim grounds, with flowerbeds and tennis courts. The ruined château is inaccessible, but, floodlit at night, picturesque by day, it dominates the landscape. When its seven great towers were repaired in the 16th century, and a now-ruined bridge and impressive entrance gate added, it must have dwarfed the Hostellerie, but in the 18th century, by order of Philippe of Orleans, much of it was demolished and the stones taken to build the Palais-Royal in Paris.

Inside the Hostellerie are a formal sitting room, a delightful, low-beamed Michelin-starred restaurant, and comfortable, elegant bedrooms in different styles, all panelled with lovely fabrics. The principal bedrooms in the main part of the house have high ceilings, tall shuttered windows overlooking the countryside, antique furniture, and chandeliers. They are reached by an impressive carved wooden staircase. On the floor above, little winding passageways and narrow flights of steps connect charming dormered rooms, decorated in pastel chintzes. One suite has two bedrooms, an enormous jacuzzi on a dais, a sitting room, and impressive views of wooded hillsides and the château ruins. There are diminutive round rooms in the tower, and huge lofty rooms in the massive rafters of the former granary. These have contemporary furniture and modern marble bathrooms. There is even a ground-floor bedroom with ramps, well-spaced furniture, extra wide doorways and a specially designed bathroom to accommodate any guest confined to a wheelchair. Given such a wide choice of rooms, it is advisable when booking to specify the desired size and furnishing of your bedroom, and to ask how many steps must be climbed to reach it.

Crayfish were a memorable feature of my delicious dinner, which also included an excellent game pie, a refreshing sorbet made from special champagne brandy, a dish of three different fillets – lamb, beef, and veal – an interesting selection of cheeses on a large trolley, a crunchy *croquant* trimmed with raspberries and strawberries, and a variety of petits fours and chocolates with the coffee. A splendid breakfast appeared next day served on a pink linen cloth on a large silver tray, with crested Limoges china and a posy of fresh flowers. Both accommodation and food are in the grand manner at the Hostellerie du Château.

The stately entrance front and dining room are shown opposite; one of the glamorous painted bathrooms appears above.

HOSTELLERIE DU CHÂTEAU, 02130 Fère-en-Tardenois. **Tel.** 23 82 21 13. **Telex** 145 526F. **Owners** The Blot family. **Closed** Jan. and Feb. **Rooms** 23 (incl. 9 suites), all with bathrooms (some with showers and/or jacuzzi), direct-dial phone, color TV, 1 room on ground floor. **Facilities** Sitting room, restaurant, gardens and woodland, tennis court, helicopter landing, conference facilities. **Re**strictions None. **Terms** Deluxe. **Credit cards** Access, Amex, Diners, Visa. **Getting there** A4, D1 dir. Soissons, R on D310 to Fère-en-Tardenois, then 3 km N on D967. 110 km. **Of local interest** Champagne trail; Reims. **Whole day expeditions** Valley of the Marne river; Paris. **Lunching out** Restaurant Boyer, Les Crayères, Reims (see p. 33); Assiette Champenoise, Châlons-sur-Vesle.

Deep in Champagne country

The town of Reims lies at the heart of the vineyards from whose grapes champagne is made. The Romans dug cellars deep into the limestone beneath the city, storing their wines in the cool, even temperatures underground, and it is in these cellars that Restaurant Boyer keeps its wines today.

A magnificent château owned by Pommery, one of the great champagne houses, has been entrusted by them to a local, internationally renowned chef and restaurateur, Gérard Boyer. Helped by his father, who first established the family name in culinary circles, and his elegant blonde wife, Elyane, he has created an outstanding hotel. Standing in beautiful park-like grounds which isolate it from the busy city traffic swirling round its walls, this graceful cream-colored stone building has become one of France's most renowned establishments, and the comfort of its spacious bedrooms matches the delicate perfection of its cuisine.

The hotel's splendid ironwork gates lead to an imposing porticoed entrance and a pillared marble hall, from which a fine staircase with an ornately wrought bronze balustrade curves gracefully up to the tapestried landing. Off this lead the vast but inviting and tastefully furnished bedrooms. My fresh and attractive panelled room had dark blue velvet couch and chairs, framed prints of birds of paradise, and pale blue bedcover. There were large white lamps, a brass bedstead and a walk-in clothes closet with a floor-to-ceiling mirror. The bathroom was marble and lavish, with excellent toiletries and a white towelling robe.

Downstairs, the bar has a *fin-de-siècle* charm created by polished mahogany and palm trees, studded leather armchairs, and dark green walls hung with prints of game birds. It is an agreeable place to sit and sip a pre-dinner glass of champagne from an impressive selection, priced with restraint, and to nibble the particularly good tiny spiced olives.

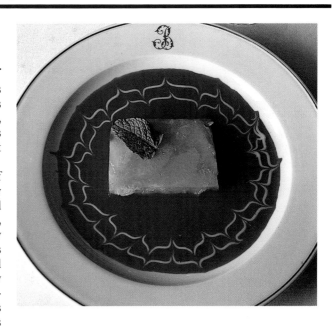

Dinner was served in the panelled dining room, lit by branched silver candelabra on every table. It was a memorable experience. Each course arrived under a silver dome which bore the house motif of a vine leaf. A superbly fragrant mouthful of wild wood-mushrooms and asparagus tips was followed by scallops in a saffron sauce rich with lobster. Morsels of grilled salmon, sea bass, and halibut were presented in a sharper sauce, accented with black and red caviar. A tiny cup of almost Oriental consommé with a hint of fresh ginger cleared the palate for venison, served with a juicily ripe fig, red cabbage, and a selection of perfect vegetables. The meal concluded with a gratin of fresh strawberries in a raspberry coulis, excellent coffee, and petits fours. A visit to Restaurant Boyer, true to its Michelin three-star status, is worth even a lengthy journey.

The stylish dining room (opposite) overlooks the huge garden. It attracts gourmets from far and wide, who come to sample Gérard Boyer's food (above). Overleaf: the elegant main staircase and a peep into the celebrated cellars.

RESTAURANT BOYER, Les Crayères, 64 boulevard Henry Vasnier, 51100 Reims. **Tel.** 26 82 80 80. **Telex** BOYER 830 959F. **Owners** Pommery. **Manager** Gérard Boyer. **Closed** 23 Dec.–11 Jan. Restaurant closed all day Mon. and Tues. lunch. **Rooms** 16 double (incl. 1 suite), all with bathroom (some with shower), direct-dial phone, radio, TV, minibar. **Facilities** Bar, terrace, 2 dining rooms, elevator, large landscaped gardens, tennis court. Golf nearby by arrangement. Helicopter landing by arrangement. Locked parking (fee). **Restrictions** None. **Terms** Deluxe. **Credit cards** All major cards. **Getting there** From Paris, A4. 135 km. **Of local interest** Visits to wine cellars and vineyards; Champagne trail; cathedral. **Whole day expeditions** Paris; small villages along Marne river. **Lunching out** Cheval Blanc, Sept Saulx; Auberge du Grand Cerf, Montchenot; Assiette Champenoise, Châlons-sur-Vesle.

10 Royal Champagne

Champillon-Bellevue
Champagne

Amid the vineyards

In autumn the vineyards make a golden sea between the browns and greens of the hillsides and the small villages dotted along the winding course of the river Marne. Royal Champagne is a hostelry built in aptly named Bellevue, with a superb view over the vineyards. It was a posting inn on one of the main roads of France, and Napoleon is said to have changed horses here. By the 1870s it had become what is known as a *guinguette*, a rustic café frequented by visitors from Epernay. The large barn in which they drank and danced is now a delightful restaurant; the orchestra that played for them sat on the same balcony that overlooks the room today.

The inn is named for one of Louis XV's cavalry regiments, the Royal Champagne, and its small cosy sitting room is lined with mementos of the time and contemporary prints of all the regiments. In one glass case are model soldiers, in another an authentic cocked hat, tall thigh boots, and a brace of pistols. A mounted cavalryman is engraved on the inn's glassware, and appears on its china and on the inn sign. Also in evidence is of course champagne, to be seen on display in the entrance hall: the wine list offers 140 different choices. Moët et Chandon have links with the inn, and it was here that they entertained to lunch Queen Elizabeth, the Queen Mother. What exactly was on the menu that day is not revealed, but she must surely have enjoyed her meal, judging by the excellence of the charcoal-grilled red snapper, chicken cooked in champagne, and smooth *marc* sorbet on which I dined.

This has always been a bustling, lively place. In summer a convivial and generous breakfast buffet is set out for guests, and at lunchtime throughout the year groups of wine enthusiasts touring the vineyards pause here to eat and to sample champagnes. There are additional dining rooms, all with martial names (such as the Salon des Fusils, complete with a display

of muzzle-loading muskets), for conferences and meetings or weddings and celebrations. Manager Marcel Dellinger, enterprising and enthusiastic, has occasionally exchanged members of staff with London's Dorchester Hotel, and keeps a keen eye on his efficient and helpful team. He will arrange private visits to the local vineyards, to see their cellars and to sample their wines, if so requested, and is very knowledgeable about local history.

Bedrooms are arranged motel-style, away from the comings and goings of the restaurant. These quiet, charmingly-furnished rooms, some with small sitting rooms, have a tasteful mix of antique and modern furnishings, fresh flowery fabrics, large tiled bathrooms, and plenty of hanging space. A bowl of fresh fruit awaits guests, whose cars can conveniently be parked in front of their doors, and the view – a panorama of vineyards – is splendid. At night, shutters are snugly wound down, and all is peaceful.

Well-managed and beautifully situated, this lively inn is a less formal alternative to the grandeur of nearby châteaux-hotels.

Mementos of Louis XV's cavalry are displayed in the salon (opposite, above). No visitor should leave without sampling some local champagne. One of the pleasant bedrooms is shown above.

ROYAL CHAMPAGNE, 51160 Champillon-Bellevue. **Tel.** 26 52 87 11/26 51 11 51. **Telex** 830 111F. **Manager** Marcel Dellinger. **Closed** 3 weeks in Jan. **Rooms** 23 (incl. 1 suite), all with bathroom (many with wall shower; 2 without tub), direct-dial phone, TV, minibar. **Facilities** Sitting room, restaurant, 4 other function/conference rooms, view. **Restrictions** None. **Terms** Moderate. **Credit cards** All major cards. **Getting there** From Paris, A4 to Reims, exit St Rémi, via route touristique 26 km. dir. Epernay (or train to Epernay; courtesy car will collect, by arrangement). 135 km. **Of local interest** Epernay; Marne valley and champagne trail; Reims; hotel can arrange private visits to vineyards, with winetasting. **Whole day expeditions** More lengthy exploration of above; private visit to museum of Dom Perignon; Paris. **Lunching out** Restaurant Boyer, Reims (see p. 33); Cheval Blanc, Sept Daulx; Auberge du Grand Cerf, Montchenot.

A château in the Loire valley

One of the great delights for visitors to France, and indeed for the French themselves, has always been a leisurely tour along the valley of the Loire, sampling its wines and visiting its magnificent châteaux. Between Blois and Tours, the river is wide and peaceful. Two kilometers above it is the Domaine des Hauts de Loire, a perfect place from which to explore the area.

Built at the end of the 18th century, on the site of an ancient nobleman's hunting lodge, between vineyards and woods, this hotel is itself a miniature château. Its long facade of tall windows with louvered shutters, flanked by a square tower at each end, is fronted by a terrace brilliant with urns of flowers and mirrored in a small lake on which swans glide peacefully. On the other side is a round turret with a roof tall and pointed like a witch's hat. Beyond is a range of stables and barns. The whole building is smothered in creeper which turns a brilliant scarlet at the end of summer. The interior does not disappoint: there is an elegant hall, a formal drawing room with chandeliers, and a long beamed dining room where yellow napery and fresh flowers adorn all the tables. A staircase with an ancient polished wooden banister spirals gently upwards from the hall to wide corridors and spacious, tastefully decorated bedrooms.

The Domaine des Hauts de Loire reminded me very much of an English country house hotel. When the Bonnigal family, who have been hoteliers for four generations, acquired the building, it had been for long neglected. During the next five years, with loving care they gradually restored this graceful period house. Mother and daughter-in-law worked with local seamstresses to sew bedcovers and draperies, the whole family searched out local antiques, and each charming bedroom was individually furnished.

One of the square tower rooms has painted rafters, a four-poster bed, and views in three directions over the countryside. There are ground-floor rooms in the converted stable block for the less agile. I was shown to my room at the top of another tower by a warmly welcoming Madame Bonnigal. The room had deep dormer windows, ancient massive beams, a wide bed (which proved to be extremely comfortable), a gold carpet and a big white couch. An archway led through to a bathroom, with attractive gold and bronze wallpaper, and equipped with thick fluffy peach towels. The afternoon tea I had requested arrived in a delicate Limoges pot on a silver tray complete with silver strainer.

Dinner, supervised by Monsieur Bonnigal, was extremely good and served with style. The fixed price menu included complimentary local wine, and there was an *à la carte* selection of other dishes offering further delicious local specialities. After a peaceful night's sleep I woke to birdsong and a splendid breakfast. I found this a most civilized hotel, embodying the finest traditions of gracious and welcoming hospitality.

The hotel is mirrored in its own calm lake (opposite); its tower conceals some attractive bedrooms (above).

DOMAINE DES HAUTS DE LOIRE, route de Herbault Mesland, 41150 Onzain. **Tel.** 54 20 72 57. **Telex** 751 547F. **Owners** The Bonnigal family. **Closed** 1 Dec.–15 Mar. **Rooms** 23 (incl. 4 suites), all with bathroom (incl. hand showers), direct-dial phone, color TV. **Facilities** Drawing room, restaurant, lake with fishing, extensive grounds with woodland walks, tennis, helicopter landing, ballooning and helicopter tours by arrangement, conference facilities in stable block. **Restrictions** No dogs. **Terms** Expensive. **Credit cards** All major cards. **Getting there** From Paris, A10 to Orleans and Blois. Exit Blois, in dir. of Tours. Drive approx 20 km. on N152 and take D1 R to Onzain. 197 km. **Of local interest** Châteaux of Blois, Amboise and Tours; Loire valley. **Whole day expeditions** Châteaux of Azay-le-Rideau, Beaugency, Chambord, Chenonceaux, Villandry; Romanesque church of Saint-Benoit-sur-Loire; vineyards with wine-tasting. **Lunching out** Auberge Jeanne de Laval, Les Rosiers-sur-Loire; Domaine de Beauvoir, Luynes; La Caillère, Cande-sur-Beuvron.

Twenties chic

On the very edge of a wide plateau, looking down over a steep drop to the wooded valley of the river Indre, stands Château d'Artigny, once the private domain of a famous French *parfumeur* of the 1920s, François Coty. A château had always stood on this site, but Coty disdained the 19th-century turreted extravaganza he found there, and, having demolished it, built his own instead. The result was this pale golden 1920s château, built around a glorious long wide gallery with a gently curving staircase at one end and at the other a gilded and ornate music room, still used for concerts. A circular restaurant with an imposing view glitters in green and gold under a sparkling chandelier. It spills over into a vast oblong room, which has a marble serving table running down one wall. A lofty bar, panelled in cream painted wood, has an enormous mirror over a wide fireplace and an impressive array of bottles. Upstairs are conference rooms, and the superb Rotunda, whose ceiling is painted with a *trompe l'oeil* depiction of M. Coty, leaning over a balcony, accompanied by guests – who include famous painters, dancers, maharajas and, it is said, his mistress – all dressed for a costume ball. The former family apartments have been divided into resplendent suites, some with vast marble bathrooms. Even the chapel, at the end of the formal gardens, has been converted into attractive and individual pillared duplex rooms.

My room overlooked the gardens and fountains, which were floodlit at night. Huge fitted closets swallowed up my clothes – they could easily have accommodated the contents of several giant steamer trunks. There was a pretty blue bedcover and matching curtains, attractive Chinese bedside lamps, and a small glittering chandelier. A blue tiled bathroom had an excellent shower and stacks of big white towels. Room service was extremely fast.

Dinner is a formal event, the service is polished and professional, and the elaborate food well merits its Michelin-starred status. I enjoyed lobster ravioli in a coral pink sauce, rack of lamb with a sauce flavored with truffles, and featherlight hot bitter chocolate and kumquat soufflé. The manager, Alain Rabier, pauses by each table for a word with his guests.

A jogging track has been thoughtfully marked in the grounds, and walks are noted on a small map. There are tennis courts and a pool, heated during the season, and fishing in the Indre from a pavilion on the river. The hotel can even arrange for guests to tour the Loire châteaux from the air.

This is another of the fine buildings that René Traversac has saved from its post-World War II decay. Restored to its former impressive luxury, with wide corridors and spacious rooms, it is the ideal venue for conferences and reunions, having modern lecture rooms tucked away out of sight and pleasant grounds where guests can stroll at leisure. The individual guest is equally well cared for, as I can vouch: this hotel, though very much in the grand manner, is excellently and efficiently run, and a pleasure to visit.

This sumptuous hotel embodies the splendors of the gilded 1920s: in the Rotunda painted figures in fancy dress look down at today's visitors (above).

CHÂTEAU D'ARTIGNY, Montbazon, 37250 Veigne. **Tel.** 47 26 24 24. **Telex** 750 900F. **Owner** Grandes Etapes Françaises (René Traversac). **General Manager** Alain Rabier. **Closed** 29 Nov.– 9 Jan. **Rooms** 53 (incl. 7 suites), all with bathroom (with wall showers), direct-dial phone, TV on request. **Facilities** Music room, Rotunda, restaurant, bar, gallery, gardens, park, walks, fishing, table tennis, 1-hole golf putting practice, tennis, swimming pool, boules, helicopter landing, flying/helicopter/balloon tours by arrangement, extensive conference facilities. **Restrictions** None. **Terms** Expensive. **Credit card** Visa. **Getting there** From Paris A10 through Tours, Montbazon exit. After 7 km. on N1, turn sw on to D17 for 2 km. 250 km. **Of local interest** Indre river valley; châteaux of Loches, Azay-le-Rideau (belonged to US War of Independence hero La Fayette); Cormery abbey. **Whole day expeditions** Loire valley and châteaux. **Lunching out** Le Choiseul, Amboise; Domaine de Beauvois, Luynes.

Luxury for the bon vivant

The main road into Joigny runs parallel with the river Yonne. On one side are ancient houses whose gardens run down to the river banks, on the other is what used to be a modest restaurant, started by the mother of Michel Lorain. This he has now transformed, with the help of his attractive blonde wife, Jacqueline, into a three-star Michelin hotel of international repute. The heavy plate-glass doors of the entrance lead to a hallway which has a display of house wines and bottled olives, preserves and conserves elegantly packaged to bear home as trophies or gifts. There are plain, pleasant bedrooms in this building more modestly priced than the magnificent new rooms in the historic houses on the other side of the Route National 6. To reach these luxury apartments, you descend in the elevator and pass along an underground passage, specially dug for this purpose, where antiquities discovered during excavation are displayed. The rooms, reached by another elevator, are as lavish as any self-indulgent bon vivant could wish: large, designer decorated, and most with wide, flower-decked balconies overlooking the peaceful river and trees beyond. Each bedroom is different. Some have exposed beams and antiques, all are panelled in gorgeous fabrics, and their sumptuous bathrooms have excellent showers and are well stocked with toiletries and thick towelling robes. On the ground floor are a glamorous heated pool, a barrel-vaulted bar, and a convenient lock-up garage.

The stone-flagged restaurant is sophisticated, with panelled walls and splendid flower arrangements. The majestic menu has delicate illustrations of the elaborately presented food of other times. Tables are well spaced; my neighbors were accompanied by an enormous German Shepherd dog which ate steak from a silver bowl with dignity, then curled up with a sigh to await the end of its owners' more extensive meal as it monitored my movements with a steady amber gaze. Selecting the gourmet menu, which allowed me to sample small portions of many different dishes, I began with a panache of game birds, foie gras and onions confit, lightly smoked sea bass with caviar, and lobster with wild mushrooms. Veal was sharpened with limes, wild duck served pink and juicy, with three sorts of cabbage, green, white, and red, each differently seasoned and spiced. Some local cheeses ripe to perfection, a rich chocolate dessert and a passionfruit sorbet completed an impeccable meal. The service was unobtrusive and swift. Michel Lorain himself appeared briefly to greet his guests at the end of the meal. His son Jean-Michel is now in the kitchens, the third generation to follow the family tradition.

An extremely comfortable night, and breakfast on the terrace overlooking the river, was followed by a shower whose needlepoint jets – from every direction – quickly jolted me into alert wakefulness.

This is not a hotel for people counting their pennies, but an excellent place to break a journey north or south if luxury and fine cuisine are what you are seeking.

The luxury apartments at this hotel provide a splendid view over the river Yonne (opposite, above). Bathrooms gleam in marble and chrome; Michel Lorain's cuisine is unforgettable (above).

LA CÔTE SAINT JACQUES, 14 Faubourg de Paris, 89300 Joigny. **Tel.** 86 62 09 70. **Telex** SAINJAC 801 458F. **Owner** Michel Lorain. **Closed** All January. **Rooms** 30. 15 luxury rooms (incl. 8 suites), all with bathroom (incl. wall shower), air conditioning, radio, direct-dial phone, color TV, and minibar. There are also 15 simpler rooms above the restaurant, all with bathroom, direct-dial phone, color TV and minibar. **Facilities** Sitting hall, bar, restaurant, heated indoor pool, elevators, lock-up garage (fee), tennis 1 km. Mooring for guests arriving by boat. **Restrictions** None. **Terms** Deluxe. **Credit cards** All major. **Getting there** From Paris, A6, exit Auxerre Nord, 26 km N on N6. 146 km. **Of local interest** Auxerre cathedral, town and abbey church; hunting; private visits to vineyards of Chablis. **Whole day expeditions** Vézelay church; valley of Cousin river; Tanlay château; Pontigny; Château St Fargeau; Avallon. **Lunching out** L'Espérance, Saint-Père-sous-Vézelay (see p. 45); La Petite Auberge, Vaux.

Culinary masterpieces

Marc Meneau comes from the village of Saint-Père. His father made harness for horses, his mother ran a small café-grocery. When he took over the café in 1970 he decided to try his hand at cooking. Self-taught, he began by making pancakes, but finding he had a real gift for creating new recipes, branched out into more exciting fare. His fame spread, and he is today one of France's top chefs, with three stars from Michelin and extravagant praise from Gault-Millau. He has even been asked to create special gourmet food for French astronauts to eat in space, as well as for explorers and mountaineers to enjoy on their earth-bound expeditions.

L'Espérance is a charming country house, set among fields, orchards, and streams in the ancient village of Saint-Père. Twin flights of steps, bordered with pots of scarlet geraniums and white daisies, curve up to meet at the front door, which opens into a gracious hall. A glittering boutique leads to a comfortable sitting room with open fire and pastel decor, and on to the glamorous conservatory-bar. This has square soft leather chairs, rows of bottles, and a white grand piano which, unnervingly, automatically plays by itself, as though with invisible fingers.

The restaurant is also in a modern conservatory overlooking the garden, filled with exotic greenery, double-glazed and draught-free. Marc Meneau's cooking is original and exciting. One of his specialities, *cromesquis*, little deep-fried cubes filled with liquid foie gras, must be eaten in one mouthful, and without talking. An unfortunate young man at the next table unwisely tried in mid-mouthful to comment on their excellence to his pretty blonde companion, with spectacular results. Very fresh turbot was delicious, tender pigeons' breasts were served with mushrooms wrapped in spinach, and an excellent salad. There were superb local cheeses, and a pineapple millefeuille was accompanied by a pineapple rum punch sorbet. An astonishing selection of handmade petits fours arrived with the coffee

on an antique gilded crystal dish. Fish is brought every day from the Paris markets, vegetables are grown in the field beside L'Espérance, and fresh herbs in its garden. The excellent wine list is well-balanced, with some outstanding (if extravagantly priced) burgundies.

Marc and his elegant wife Françoise also own a charming old mill house on the other side of the village, with somewhat larger bedrooms and more countrified decor than the smaller, sophisticated rooms in L'Espérance, where I slept. My bedroom had creaking floors, a marble and blue-tiled super-modern bathroom, Cocteau prints, blue peony-patterned bedspread, and scarlet velvet antique chairs. Breakfast was one of the best I've had in France – a selection of fruit, fresh breads and cheeses on a big wooden tray with pretty matching pink, white and blue flowered china and cloth (the same may be purchased from the boutique).

Behind the scenes, the kitchens are as modern and magnificent as the restaurant, with vast copper pans and immaculate tiled surfaces: a fit setting for such an outstanding master of creative culinary delights.

Inside and out, L'Espérance provides a delightful rural setting for Marc Meneau's gastronomic feats. The conservatory bar and restaurant are shown overleaf; opposite is a truly sumptuous breakfast.

L'ESPÉRANCE, 89450 Saint-Père-sous-Vézelay. **Tel.** 86 33 20 45. **Telex** 800 005F. **Owners** Marc and Françoise Meneau. **Closed** Early Jan.–early Feb. Restaurant only, all day Tues. and Wed. lunch. **Rooms** 21, all with bathroom (incl. wall showers), radio, direct-dial phone, color TV. **Facilities** Sitting room, bar, restaurant, boutique, small lake and gardens at Moulin, helicopter landing. Restrictions None. **Terms** Deluxe. **Credit cards** Amex, Diners, Visa. **Getting there** From Paris, A6 to Avallon, D957 to Saint-Père. 217 km. **Of local interest** Romanesque church of Vézelay; Avallon. **Whole day expeditions** Dijon; Beaune; Autun; Nature Park of Morvan; Chablis region. **Lunching out** La Côte d'Or, Saulieu.

A taste of Alsace

I have for years enjoyed the wines from Alsace supplied by the firm of Dopff and Irion of Riquewihr, but it was not until I decided to drop in on these wine merchants en route to Switzerland one year that I discovered the charm of this remote corner of France.

Between the Vosges mountains and the river Rhine, often invaded and constantly fought over since Roman times and probably before, Alsace has nevertheless kept its distinctive character, and many of its historic buildings have survived. Strasbourg, home of the European Parliament, whose glorious cathedral is rich with superb carving and stained glass, has also a picturesque medieval quarter, as has Colmar, home of many art treasures. Behind them are the Vosges foothills, covered in vineyards and a whole chain of medieval small towns and villages, linked by the meandering *route du vin*, the wine trail. They have steep cobbled streets, and wooden-beamed houses with red tiled roofs sometimes bearing the nest of a white stork. On the hilltops above are the massive castle strongholds to which the villagers fled in troubled times, and the *route des crêtes*, the mountain road which links mountain summits via valleys and forests, providing panoramic views for those with strong nerves and good brakes.

Riquewihr is the most picturesque of the villages, and therefore tends to be crowded in summer. I noted that local specialities – foie gras, sausages, *choucroute* (spicy cabbage), Munster cheese, *kougelhof* (fruity cake), raspberry liqueur – were offered in its small inns, though they are not always obtainable in grander establishments. Rouffach, an equally ancient town, if less dramatic than Riquewihr, has the great advantage of possessing the Château d'Isenbourg, a fine turreted château hotel.

There has been a castle here since at least 660. The 13th-century cellars survive, and are today an impressive restaurant, hung with giant swords and shields, tapestries and pennants. Much of the rest was

alternately stormed and destroyed, then rebuilt, over the centuries.

The road to the château winds up through the vineyards, past ranges of outer buildings (which house very comfortable modern bedrooms furnished in pretty chintzes and rattan), past the tennis courts and pool, to emerge into a large courtyard with a fountain in front of the great wooden front door. The entrance hall is spacious, as are the various elegantly furnished sitting rooms and bar. Manager Daniel Dalibert encourages a house-party atmosphere and with his delightful wife and son oversees his guests' comfort. Touring information includes walking and cycling maps, and the day's weather forecast is displayed by the front door. Room service is swift, as is service in the restaurant, where the food is delicious. Bedrooms include suites with painted ceilings and antique furniture; bathrooms are luxurious, with good showers. There are superb views over the ancient little town to Germany's Black Forest beyond. This hotel is impressive and majestic, but also comfortable, professional, and caring.

From the hotel's terrace the view extends over the roof tops of Rouffach to the Black Forest in the distance. The food (above) is as stylish as the interiors (overleaf).

CHÂTEAU D'ISENBOURG, 68250 Rouffach. Tel. 89 49 63 53. **Telex** 880 819F. **Owner** Les Grandes Etapes Françaises (René Traversac). **Manager** Daniel Dalibert. **Closed** All Jan.–early Mar. **Rooms** 40 (incl. 3 suites), all with bathroom (incl wall shower), direct-dial phone, most with TV. The 8 rooms in the pavilion have minibars in addition. **Facilities** 4 sitting rooms, bar, 4 dining rooms (2 public, 2 private), conference facilities, elevator, tennis court, heated pool, helicopter landing, bicycles for hire, riding nearby. **Restrictions** None. **Terms** Expensive. **Credit cards** Access, Visa. **Getting there** From Paris, A4 to Strasbourg, A35 to Colmar, N83, turn off R to Rouffach; hotel signposted. 550 km. **Of local interest** Eco-Museum (local museum with folk art, etc.); *route du vin*; *route des crêtes*; Colmar (Unterlinden Museum); Kayserberg; Riquewihr; automobile and railroad museum at Mülhouse. **Whole day expeditions** Longer tours to any of the above; Haut-Koenigsbourg; Strasbourg (cathedral and museum). **Lunching out** Schillinger, Colmar; Auberge Père Floranc, Wettolsheim; Auberge de l'Ill, Illhäusern.

A welcoming family inn

This delightful family-run posting inn is perched on the very edge of a precipice, surrounded by meadows and woodland in which the owners sometimes see chamoix. The road climbs steeply from Poligny, rising almost 1000 feet in under 5 kilometers – which explains the huge size of the stables required when the inn was built in 1793, to accommodate replacements for exhausted carriage horses. Between the world wars it became a small café, Chez Lo-Lo, with drinks and dancing, but it was run-down when the Carrion family bought it some twenty years ago.

Monsieur Carrion had always wanted to cook (he remains invisible in the kitchens) and does so with expertise, producing interesting dishes, perfectly cooked. The menu is simple and hand-written. I chose a *salade paysanne* with a light vinaigrette, a local trout lightly flavored with rosemary, a veal escalope, and crème caramel, all cooked with fresh local ingredients. The price of this delicious meal was included in the cost of the room. The unique local *vin jaune*, little known and much underrated, has a strong taste, deep yellow color, and is excellent with spicy foods.

Breakfast in my room was set out for me on a starched cloth on a table. Delicate Limoges china had a Chinese bird and flower pattern, there was a tall silver coffee pot, and a silver rack for toast, as well as a basket of assorted breads, marmalade as well as conserves and honey.

Madame Carrion manages the accounts, and passes the long winter months working on the fine embroidery, patchwork, and drawn-thread-work which, with the well-polished local antiques, are a feature of this lovingly-cherished inn. Copper and pewter, old apothecary jars made into lamps, painted china, and a handsome grandfather clock give character to the public rooms. Bedrooms, panelled in fabric and hung with antique prints, have down-filled duvets and tiled bathrooms. One of the suites has the bed on a gallery above, beneath a double-glazed skylight whose blind rolls up so that at night you can lie in bed and admire the stars. By day, its sitting area looks out over the spectacular cliffs. The Carrions' daughter shares with her brother the friendly reception of guests and the serving of drinks and food. He, precise in a bow tie, greets guests with an elegant – even poetic – turn of phrase. Madame Carrion and her daughter both speak excellent English. An enormous black furry dog, Uriel, adds his enthusiastic greetings to guests, though desists on command.

Caught in a sudden alarming snowstorm as I crossed the mountains on my way here, I appreciated the warmth and quality of the family's hospitality, which – with the simple excellence of the food and the traditional furnishing – reminded me of a France I had known years ago, before designer decor, modern glitter and passing fashions in food obliterated many of the differences between country hotels. This quiet corner of the mountains has preserved its special rural charm.

The high plateau above Poligny is a spectacular setting for this family inn, which has exhilarating views from its garden (opposite and overleaf). Local produce and warm comfort are also memorable features.

HOSTELLERIE DES MONTS DE VAUX, 39800 Poligny. **Tel.** 84 37 12 50. **Telex** 361 493F. **Owners** The Carrion family. **Closed** End Oct.–end Dec. and all day Tuesday and Wednesday to 6 p.m. out of season. **Rooms** 10 (incl. 2 suites), all with bathroom (with hand shower), direct-dial phone, 2 with TV. **Facilities** Sitting room, restaurant, garden, field and woods, lock-up garage (fee), tennis. **Restrictions** None. **Terms** Moderate (prices include dinner and breakfast). **Credit cards** Amex, Visa, Diners.

Getting there From Paris, A6 to Beaune, N on A31, E on A36 to Dole, S on N5 via Poligny, Monts de Vaux signposted. 400 km. **Of local interest** Abbey of Baume les Messieurs; Joux forest; Poligny; Salines Royales at Arc-et-Senans. **Whole day expeditions** Besançon (citadel, museums, clock); Dole; Loue valley and waterfalls; Jura vineyards. **Lunching out** Le Paris, Arbois; Le Valentin, École Valentin, nr Besançon.

17 Troisgros

Traditional excellence revitalized

It is not often that a station hotel wins three Michelin stars, but it was as the modest Hôtel des Platanes, serving the passengers from the pink-painted Roanne station directly across the road, that the Troisgros parents in 1930 bought the hotel that was to become world-famous under their name.

The Troisgros sons, Jean and Pierre, trained in the finest French restaurants and returned in 1953 to the family hotel, renamed Les Frères Troisgros. Over the years, working from a tiny kitchen, their robust, ebullient personalities, their joy in cooking, and their notable culinary creations gained country-wide acclaim and international recognition. Sadly, Jean is no more. Though much shaken by his loss, Pierre Troisgros, joined by his son Michel, who has been trained in the most famous kitchens of today, has courageously made a new start. He has brought back vitality to the menu, continued to modernize the hotel, built enormous new kitchens with plate-glass windows, excavated a superb new cellar and a subterranean car-park, and transformed the former car-park into a charming courtyard garden. Gault-Millau has greeted this renaissance with four toques, top symbol of approval. Stocky, bearded Michel has a delightful wife, Marie-Pierre, who joins her mother-in-law, Olympe, at reception; Michel and Marie-Pierre's children form the fourth generation of Troisgros.

The menus themselves are works of art, and the dishes are richly seasoned and generous: crab and scallops perfumed with coriander; pan-fried sole served in a spring-onion-flavored sauce; duck unusually but successfully teamed with rhubarb; a whole panier of magnificent cheeses; a dazzling array of desserts and sorbets; splendid petits fours. The wine list includes superb burgundies and cognacs. Breakfast is formally served and unstinted. The trolley, graced with a starched cloth and an orchid, bore a large silver thermos of splendid coffee, a big

jug of hot milk, and a small mountain of Danish pastries, *pain-au-chocolat*, croissants, crunchy French bread, two sorts of conserves and honey – and a newspaper.

There are smaller bedrooms to the left of the hotel, linked by a glass corridor, and some overlook the gardens. I stayed in one of the amazing de-luxe duplex bedrooms above the restaurant, reached by elevator. The two-storey windows with push-button shutters looked over rooftops to the mountains of the Massif Central. A seating area had a soft leather sofa, the bed was in a dark-brown cave with carpeted floor, walls, and ceiling, with niches for lighting and books. The balcony bathroom, reached by a twisting spiral staircase, had mirrors framed in lights like a film star's, a gleaming black floor, and a forest of silk plants. Air-conditioned or centrally-heated at the turn of a control knob, double-glazed against traffic noise, here the weary traveler can relax in luxury, pampered by several generations of inimitable Troisgros.

Fine wine and fresh produce are essential elements in Pierre and Michel Troisgros's cuisine. A corner of the courtyard garden is shown opposite, above.

TROISGROS, Place de la Gare, 42300 Roanne. **Tel.** 77 71 66 97. **Telex** 307 507F. **Owner** Pierre Troisgros. **Closed** All Jan.; 4–19 Aug.; all day Tues., Wed. lunch. **Rooms** 23 (incl. 3 suites), all with bathroom (incl. wall shower), direct-dial phone, 21 with TV and minibar. **Facilities** Hall-sitting room, restaurant, bar, courtyard, garden, elevator, garage. **Restrictions** None. **Terms** Expensive. **Credit cards** All major cards. **Getting there** From Paris, A6, exit Chalon Sud, voie express to Roanne. 390 km. **Of local interest** Charlieu; Ambierle; Burgundy vineyards and villages. **Whole day expeditions** Lyon (old town and Gallo-Roman museum); longer visits to above. **Lunching out** La Poularde, Montrond-les-Bains; Leon de Lyon, Lyon.

18 Alain Chapel

Mionnay
Dombes

A sophisticated village inn

Happy the inhabitants of Lyon, with the Beaujolais vineyards on their doorstep, and a dazzling selection of culinary stars encircling their city. The Troisgros (see p. 57) at Roanne in their newly glamorous hotel; Georges Blanc in a transformed rustic retreat (see p. 63); Paul Bocuse, transatlantic commuter overseeing the French restaurant in Epcot USA and his own notable establishment at Collonges-au-Mont-d'Or (not featured in this book since not a hotel – but superb); and their colleague in the three-star Michelin league, Alain Chapel.

Like so many of the famous chefs of France, Alain Chapel is following a family tradition. In the 1930s, his parents bought La Mère Charles, then a picturesque village café (once painted by Utrillo), set beside the road to Bourg-en-Bresse and next door to the school and town hall. His father, Roger, was the chef-patron, as Alain is today. The outside of the hotel remains modest, but beyond the entrance archway is a well-manicured little garden, and heavy plate-glass doors lead into a sophisticated flagstoned entrance hall. There are particularly lovely flower arrangements everywhere; the restaurant's starched white cloths are glimpsed to the right, while to the left the hallway leads invitingly to a display of wines and conserves that may be purchased, and to a most tempting bar. Dimly lit, panelled like an English club, with huge soft dark-brown armchairs, it offers an exotic list of cocktails.

The room keys are attached to enormous champagne corks, and so are impossible to lose. The bedrooms are modest in size, though larger ones are planned, and prettily furnished in Laura Ashley flowered fabrics. In my bedroom, purple pansies and dark yellow ribbons on the white glazed-cotton bedcover were complemented by pale yellow walls and moss-green carpet. The bathroom had handmade ceramic tiles with a blue-gray glaze, and pink towels.

But it is the food that has always drawn Lyon residents as well as international travelers to this little village. Plump grains of caviar floated in the velvet-smooth asparagus soup, the delicate brill was served in a fine sauce of oysters and mussels, venison was accompanied by rich lyonnaise potatoes. I was delighted to find some robust Cantal cheese among the farm-produced selection, and rounded off my meal with a plate of assorted delicate ices and fruit sorbets. I could alas then do less than justice to the dessert trolley and *douceurs et mignardises*, all manner of delicious small sweetmeats. There is an exceptional wine list, most comprehensive, and unusual in its wide selection of madeiras and ports. A fashionable clientele is served swiftly and expertly, and Alain Chapel himself circulates briefly.

A marvellous breakfast, a quick word with Alain's chic and soignée wife Suzanne at the reception desk, and I continued my journey south, regretful to be leaving this elegant village retreat.

Three-star food and a sophisticated ambience at Alain Chapel are complimented by the rural charm of the inn and its gardens.

ALAIN CHAPEL, 01390 Mionnay. **Tel.** 78 91 82 02. **Telex** 305 605F. **Owner** Alain Chapel. **Closed** All Jan.; all day Mon; Tues. lunch (except on public holidays). **Rooms** 13, all with bathroom, direct-dial phone, TV. 6 additional larger rooms are planned. **Facilities** Sitting room, bar, helicopter landing, lock-up garage (fee). A large garden and additional private parking space are planned. **Restrictions** None. **Terms** Deluxe. **Credit cards** All major cards. **Getting there** From Paris, A6 Anse exit after Villefranche-sur-Saône, D51 to Neuville, D38/N83 towards Montany. Hotel in Mionnay village. (NB the high-speed rail service from Paris to Lyon takes only 2 hrs.) 500 km. **Of local interest** Pérouges; Lyon; Beaujolais vineyards; 13th-cent. church at Brou, the burial place of the Dukes of Savoy; Châtillon-sur-Chalaronne (picturesque village); church at Saint Paul de Varax. **Whole day expeditions** Lyon; birdwatching in Dombes region, especially in spring when the region attracts numerous migratory wildfowl. **Lunching out** Paul Bocuse, Collonges-au-Mont-d'Or.

Echoes of the Belle Epoque

The Kings of Savoy established Evian as a fashionable summer resort, attracted by the beauty of the lake and the nearby spa at Amphion. In 1790, the town's own mineral springs were discovered and Evian began to attract yet more visitors. Lord Byron and Shelley, cruising on the lake in Byron's yacht, called in at the new spa in 1816. Evian's golden age was the "Belle Epoque" of 1870 to 1914 – when it was visited by Proust – and its elegant buildings embody that leisured time. The mountains of Savoy rise steeply behind the town, and across the smooth blue waters of Lake Leman are the Swiss Alps.

La Verniaz is not one of the vast old spa hotels, but a regional wooden chalet-farmhouse with overhanging eaves, high on the hillside outside Evian. It was bought and converted at the turn of the century by a Monsieur Florinetti, who added a more sophisticated block of larger rooms yet further up the slope, and re-erected some enchanting tiny *mazots*, the old, hand-hewn chalets formerly built near each mountain farmhouse as a storage place for fodder and valuables. Since the 1930s Michelin-starred La Verniaz has been owned by the Verdier family.

I arrived in March, together with a late snowstorm that trimmed in white the surrounding mountains and chalets. In winter months the upstairs restaurant is open. At the top of a massive wooden staircase, it has heavy beams and wooden walls, and a bar at one end decorated on a golfing theme with antique clubs and cartoons. I ate my dinner sitting before a cosy log fire, and after some excellent pâté watched my steak being grilled on an antique spit worked with wooden weights. A salad, some local Reblochon cheese and a hot soufflé with *griotte* cherries and kirsch ended a tasty meal.

I stayed in the former barn, a few steps across the garden. Wooden floors creaked, but it was snug and warm, and the double-glazed balcony provided a spectacular view. There were crisp linen sheets on the bed, which was turned down for me at night, and a linen mat placed beside the bed – a courtesy perhaps learned from London's exclusive Connaught Hotel, where the owner's daughter was trained. The room had country furniture and flowery curtains, pieces of well-polished brass, and a warm tiled bathroom. A friendly cheerful girl brought me breakfast, which included sugary buns, croissants and plaited breads.

In summer the gardens come into their own. On the steep hillside, streams trickle into stone basins, and brilliant flowers bloom in place of the primroses I saw. The upstairs restaurant is closed and one downstairs is opened, together with a giant outside grill preparing barbecued foods, and the Thistle bar with over 100 whiskys. Tables and umbrellas are dotted beside pool and tennis court. In summer a relaxed and relaxing rural country club, surrounded by flowering Alpine meadows, in winter a cosy refuge: La Verniaz is a place to remember.

The view from the top of the hotel across gardens, hotel buildings and pool towards the lake beyond is shown opposite. Below is the outdoor grill restaurant (left) and the bar. The pretty bedrooms (above) are very inviting.

LA VERNIAZ, route d'Abondance, 74500 Evian-les-Bains. **Tel.** 50 75 04 90. **Telex** 385 715F. **Owners** The Verdier family. **Closed** End Nov.–early Feb. **Rooms** 36 (incl. 1 suite with fireplace), 5 chalets, all with bathroom (incl. hand shower), direct-dial phone, minibar, 12 with TV. **Facilities** Winter upstairs bar, restaurant; summer downstairs outdoor grill restaurant, indoor restaurant, bar, sitting rooms, elevator in garden block, gardens, heated pool, tennis court (others close by), golf 2 km, sailing by arrangement, 2 free lock-up garages. **Restrictions** No dogs in restaurants. **Terms** Moderate. **Credit cards** All major cards. **Getting there** From Paris, A6, either via Lyon to A43/A41, avoiding Geneva via N206/N5, or (when complete) from Macon A40 in direction of Geneva, as above. 580 km. **Of local interest** Boat trips on lake; Valley of Abondance, Abbey and cloisters; Geneva, Château of Chillon; Château de Coppet (former home of Madame de Staël); many golf courses round lake (in Switzerland). **Whole day expeditions** Switzerland; Chamonix-Mont Blanc; Annecy and lake; in winter, skiing; in summer, walking. **Lunching out** La Toque Royale (in casino), Evian; Le Prieuré, Thonon-les-Bains.

20 Georges Blanc

Vonnas
Burgundy

A hundred years of good food

You should have no problem finding Georges Blanc's luxurious rustic hideaway, since it is widely heralded by the name Georges Blanc writ large on walls with directions and distance. Entering the village of Vonnas, I parked in the square, and found myself facing a boutique and provisions shop also bearing his name. Georges's mother ran a simple village restaurant, La Mère Blanc, from which he and his elegant and efficient wife, Jacqueline, have created a glamorous and extremely comfortable hotel.

The three-star Michelin restaurant has a beamed ceiling and stone-flagged floors, tapestries, and huge open fires. The immaculately presented food is served at a very leisurely pace, but who would want to rush a meal of this caliber? It is a delight to find – in a menu the size of a local newspaper, whose cover is a patchwork of mouth-watering photographs of food – a choice not only of the chef's own creative dishes, but also delicious traditional regional specialities, so sadly often ignored – why? – by the great chefs. You may if you wish sample frogs' legs and snails, the famous Bresse pigeon and chicken, and choose from a wide selection of local cheeses and a trolley groaning with luscious desserts. Everything is immaculately presented in this riverside, flower-bedecked setting. Next morning's breakfast was served on poppy-patterned china, and included fresh fruit and tiny cheeses, freshly-baked breads, and strong good coffee.

The conservatory sitting room and bar was created from a former courtyard, and the colorful gardens win prizes for their flowers. A gleaming swimming pool has comfortable pool-side lounging chairs; there is a tennis court and pitch-and-putt golf, and space has been made for a helicopter landing pad – extremely useful for those with frenetic schedules or famous faces. A former lemonade factory at the back of the hotel has become lovely spacious duplex bedrooms with flagstone floors, stone fireplaces, antiques, and beds on wooden galleries. Every year improvements are made for guests' greater comfort, including the addition of airconditioning to all of the bedrooms. I had a modest room, fabric-hung, with a good tiled bathroom, antique prints on the walls, double glazing, and a comfortable bed.

Georges Blanc, smooth-faced and youthful, has nevertheless two sons already training to join the team. The inn was bought by their great-grandparents in 1872 to serve the farmers who came to town on market day with horse and waggon. They paused for a bowl of soup on their way in, and returned later for a hearty meal. Today's clients may be less bucolic, but they share the enthusiasm for the family Blanc's cooking that has been felt in Vonnas for well over a hundred years – a reputation which the fourth generation of the family certainly intends to maintain.

Even the flowers proudly proclaim the name of the owner and chef of this famous hotel. The food (above) is magnificent and the accommodation spacious: one of the duplex bedrooms is shown opposite.

HOTEL-RESTAURANT GEORGES BLANC, 01540 Vonnas. **Tel.** 74 50 00 10. **Telex** 380 776F. **Owner** Georges Blanc. **Closed** Early Jan.–mid Feb.; restaurant only, all day Wed. and Thurs. (except mid June–mid Sept.: open Thurs. evening). **Rooms** 30 (incl. 4 suites), all with bathroom (suites have showers), airconditioning, direct-dial phone, TV. **Facilities** Sitting room-bar, restaurant, private dining room, terrace, elevator, airconditioning throughout, gardens, river, pool, tennis court, pitch and putt, boutiques, free lock-up garage, helicopter landing. **Restrictions** None. **Terms** Deluxe. **Credit cards** All major cards. **Getting there** From Paris, A6 exit Macon Nord, N79 dir. Bourg-en-Bresse, D80 s to Vonnas. (High-speed train from Paris to Macon-Loche takes 1 hr 40 mins.) 500 km. **Of local interest** Bourg-en-Bresse; countryside with farmhouses, villages, churches. **Whole day expeditions** Beaujolais vineyards; Lyon; Perouges; Cluny. **Lunching out:** Auberge du Cep, Fleurie; Paul Bocuse, Collanges-au-Mont-d'Or.

21 Pic

A three-star welcome

Probably the best loved of all France's top chefs, Jacques Pic is smiling, pleasantly rounded, and radiates welcome, as does his equally kindly wife. Not that he is easy to track down, since he stays resolutely in his kitchens, accompanied by his bearded son and his highly-trained team, personally producing the exceptionally delicious food which has won for him the three Michelin stars also held by his father in the 1930s.

The traveler has only to turn briefly off the autoroute to the south to arrive at the door of Pic. Avenue Victor Hugo is a broad tree-lined street on the outskirts of Valence, and you must watch hard for the hotel sign on the right. You can enter through the main gate, straight into a garden that is a riot of colour, with huge earthenware pots, creepers, and tables in summer, or through the side entrance that leads into a small hall with an antique reception table. Beyond is the panelled restaurant, furnished with pale pink tablecloths and glittering silver.

Guests are greeted with suave politeness by the impeccable *maître d'hôtel* (trained in London's Connaught Hotel), seated in the garden or in the comfortably plump armchairs in the small sitting room according to season, and plied with appetisers – in my case a plaited loaf hollowed out and filled with canapés. Resisting with difficulty the multiple delicious courses of the Menu Rabelais, I began with superb lobster, served with a light vinaigrette and a salad with beetroot – a symphony of pinks and reds. This was followed by succulent turbot with wood-mushrooms, and then venison in a rich burgundy sauce, with perfect vegetables. Finally I selected from the basket-work pannier of cheeses a sharp goat cheese, and was encouraged to try several of the splendid desserts from the trolley, among which a Charlotte flavored with ginger was perhaps the most memorable.

Presidents of France, filmstars, businessmen, visitors from abroad and the local Valentinois have all enjoyed the cooking of Jacques Pic. His techniques are rooted in the recipes passed down from his grandmother, who cooked for hunters and travelers in the Auberge du Pin, high above Saint-Peray. His father, having won his third Michelin star in 1934, moved down into Valence and bought the delightful ancient house of an antique dealer, with its tree-shaded gardens. Jacques Pic beams with pleasure at the thought that his son is following in the family tradition.

A notable cellar offers a choice of outstanding wines, including the finest products of the Côtes-du-Rhone vineyards.

There is space for no more than four simple bedrooms of varying sizes (two of them suites) at the top of the steep staircase. They are all comfortable, with good bathrooms, carved provincial antique furniture and tasteful framed prints. Bookings must be made far in advance to secure a room, and dedicated gourmets sometimes settle for a night in a modern motel, such as the nearby Novotel, in order to enjoy eating in the charming house of a man who clearly cooks not only because it is his livelihood, but because he enjoys it so much.

The world comes to Valence to sample Jacques Pic's superb food, served in the elegant dining room (above) or on the terrace in summer (opposite). Overleaf: a sitting room (top left) and bedroom (bottom right), both typical of the hotel's comfortable accommodation. The gardens are charming, but it is the cuisine that is unforgettable.

RESTAURANT PIC, 285 avenue Victor Hugo, 26000 Valence. **Tel.** 75 44 15 32. **Telex** None. **Owner** Jacques Pic. **Closed** Feb. school holidays, 3 weeks in August, all day Wed. and Sun. nights. **Rooms** 4 (incl. 2 suites), all with bathroom, direct-dial phone, TV. **Facilities** Sitting room, garden, lock-up garage (fee). **Restrictions** None. **Terms** Expensive. **Credit cards** Amex, Diners, Visa. **Getting there** From Paris, A6/A7 to exit Valence-Sud, follow signs to av. Victor Hugo, hotel on R. 560 km. **Of local interest** Côtes du Rhône vineyards; Valence cathedral and old city. **Whole day expeditions** Vercors nature park and mountains. **Lunching out** Chabran, Pont-de-l'Isere.

Deep in the Dordogne

In spring, a carpet of sweetly-scented wild violets covers the lawn at the Vieux Logis. Bernard Giraudel-Destord told me that they had been the favorite flower of his father-in-law, and had suddenly appeared, like some small consoling miracle, on the first spring after his death. The Giraudel-Destord family has lived in this house for 400 years. Built on the site of a priory, it was their country home, their main residence being in Bergerac, and it served to house also their farm manager and labourers, in different wings and cottages.

The large barn which today forms the restaurant was built over 150 years ago to dry tobacco, and was then converted to hold livestock in stalls that still remain, the fodder being stored on the balconied upper floor. It made a very pleasant setting for a candlelit dinner, after a drink in the rustic bar bright with red-checked gingham. The menu is reasonably priced; fresh local produce and traditional recipes are the basis for tasty dishes, simply prepared, and served by friendly local girls. The sitting room to the left of the entrance hall has very much the feeling of a country parlor. The fireplace has a massive fireback and a mantlepiece crowded with ornaments; a musket hangs on the wall, and the country antique furniture glows with long years of loving care.

Le Vieux Logis was first transformed into a hotel by Bernard Giraudel-Destord's mother, a notable regional cook, and he has continued to convert further bedrooms, some tucked up under the eaves, some large and spacious, all furnished in striking designer fabrics with rich provincial patterns from Souleiado. My bedroom, reached by walking through the gardens, looked out over the beds of flowers and little swift clear brook – complete with small fish and crossed by two small bridges and a row of stepping stones – to the fields and a small church beyond. It had solid mahogany twin beds, with a half-canopy over, and massive pieces of antique provincial

furniture. There were attractive pieces of china and copper, and a sitting area with a table and chairs. The decor was in shades of blue, with a creamy-white fitted carpet. The bathroom had white tiles and plenty of big fluffy white towels.

There is a further enormous fortified 11th-century church in the village, and in the square in front of it old men in berets sit at the tables of an outdoor café, impassively watching the world go by. The Dordogne valley, with its wide, winding, tree-shaded river, is rich in ancient villages, picturesque churches, castles, caves, and prehistoric sites. The paintings in the famous Lascaux caves are alas too fragile for public visits, but those in the Font-de-Gaume are on view.

Le Vieux Logis, filled with generations of family possessions, still feels very much somebody's home. Helpful with touring information, ready to provide picnic hampers, it is, unusually for France, open every day all year round, and makes a marvellously peaceful base from which to explore the fascinating countryside of the Dordogne.

Beautiful fabrics and exposed beams in the bedrooms (opposite) create an atmosphere at once sophisticated and rural. Fresh produce of the Dordogne (above) is the basis for the traditional dishes served here. Overleaf: a view of the ancient hotel buildings from the garden.

LE VIEUX LOGIS, 24510 Trémolat. **Tel.** 53 22 80 06. **Telex** 541 025F. **Owner** Bernard Giraudel-Destord. **Open** Every day, all year. **Rooms** 19 (incl. 3 suites), all with bathroom (incl. wall shower), direct-dial phone, TV, minibar. **Facilities** 2 sitting rooms, bar, 2 restaurants, small conference facilities, gardens with stream, helicopter landing. **Restrictions** None. **Terms** Moderate. **Credit cards** All major cards. **Getting there** From Paris, A10 to Poitiers. Take road to Angoulême, then to Périgueux and from there to Le Bugue. Take road to Limeil and from there to Trémolat. 565 km. **Of local interest** Dordogne valley, villages, etc. River sports (water-skiing, etc.). **Whole day expeditions** *Bastides*, villages fortified by the English in 13th-century wars – Monpazier, Biron, etc.; Eyzies-de-Tayac (prehistoric sites); medieval town of Sarlat; Bordeaux vineyards. **Lunching out** Le Cyrano, Bergerac; Le Centenaire, Cro-Magnon, Eyzies-de-Tayac.

In an ancient watermill

Tucked beside a mountain stream, in glorious countryside not far from the valley of the Dordogne, is the Hostellerie du Moulin du Roc, an enchanting inn created from an ancient watermill built to crush walnuts for their oil. The wheels and cogs, massive beams, and complicated machinery are still here, polished and gleaming, incorporated into the charming sitting rooms, which are furnished with antiques and pretty fabrics, cheered by big open log fires, and filled with fresh flowers.

The bedrooms are equally fascinating, some with four-poster beds, most with beams and sloping floors and ceilings; all are snug and comfortable. Mine had a wide bed with an ornate painted Spanish headboard, pink sheets and blankets with a heavy white cotton cover, and a television and minibar discreetly concealed in a handsome period cupboard. There was even a hand-hewn crib on which to put my bags. Two walls were covered in dark pink linen fabric, two were the smoothly hewn natural limestone blocks from which the mill is built. Lying in bed, I looked out over tiled roofs and a wooded hillside to the square tower of the local church. The tiny window in my impeccable modern bathroom was almost at floor-level, overlooking the stream and the busy comings and goings of a yellow wagtail nest-building on the opposite bank.

As you enter the hotel through the little garden spilling over with bright flowers, some planted in round black antique iron cauldrons, the first thing your eyes fall upon is a glass tank of live lobsters, lugubriously waving claws and feelers. Now brown and purple, they will soon miraculously be transformed to their more familiar scarlet, under the watchful eye of Solange Gardillou, one of France's few lady chefs to be honored with two Michelin stars and three red toques from Gault-Millau. While her charming husband Lucien presides over hotel and restaurant, this slim blonde master chef creates her marvels. I much enjoyed a perfectly seasoned Salade du Moulin, embellished with foie gras and smoked goose, followed by fresh salmon in a delicate pink sauce sharpened by spicy pink peppercorns. Delicious local cheeses and an airy confection of spun sugar crowning a fragile pastry basket filled with homemade sorbets and sliced fresh fruits concluded a notable meal. Breakfast the next morning consisted of freshly baked breads and a silver pot of excellent coffee brought up by a smiling girl in traditional local costume, her blonde hair plaited in a thick braid down her back.

The whole hotel is a treasury of fascinating antiques, discovered by the Gardillous in forays all over Europe. Every available corner of the public rooms and the bedrooms is packed with delightful "objets."

Solange, a self-taught chef, told me that she is delighted now to have one son with her in the kitchen, with a second learning administration. She and her husband are happy to think that their much-loved mill, rescued from a ruin and cherished over twenty years, will eventually pass into equally caring hands.

A garden by a mountain stream, an inviting dining room (opposite) and imaginatively furnished bedrooms (above) are some of the pleasures of this family hotel.

HOSTELLERIE DU MOULIN DU ROC, 24530 Champagne-de-Belair. **Tel.** 53 54 80 36. **Telex** 571 555F MOULROC. **Owners** Lucien and Solange Gardillou. **Closed** 15 Nov.–15 Dec., 15 Jan.–5 Feb.; restaurant only closed all day Tues. and Wed. lunch. **Rooms** 14, all with bathroom, direct-dial phone, TV, minibar. **Facilities** 2 sitting rooms, restaurant, terrace, helicopter landing, swimming pool, tennis. Golf and riding nearby, by arrangement. **Restrictions** None.

Terms Moderate. **Credit cards** All major cards. **Getting there** From Paris, A10 to Poitiers, N10 to Angoulême, D959 to Brantôme. 450 km. **Of local interest** Boating, fishing, walking; Dordogne valley and its picturesque villages; Eyzies-de-Tayac (prehistoric sites). **Whole day expeditions** Bordeaux and Cognac vineyards. **Lunching out** Moulin de l'Abbaye, Brantôme; L'Oison, Perigueux.

Gastronomic glories

Tired after the long drive to the far south-west corner of France, I wondered what could possibly be so special about Les Prés d'Eugénie that is should draw people from all over France, indeed from all over the world. Its Michelin classification of three stars means "worth a special journey." Was it? Without question.

Eugénie-les-Bains takes its name from the Empress Eugénie, Spanish wife of Napoleon III, who first made fashionable this sleepy little spa town in the foothills of the Pyrenees. Now the perfection of Michel Guérard's cooking and the lavish magnificence of his hotel and spa have restored its *éclat*. The hotel, with ornate wrought-iron balconies and broad shady terraces, stands amid groves of pine and plane trees. Its grounds contain palms, orange and banana trees, magnolias, roses, and bamboo, as well as a huge herb garden, gleaming white statues of nymphs, smooth green lawns, an azure pool, a gazebo, and tennis courts. The elegant interior, designed by Michel's wife, Christine, has clean-cut, simple lines. The southern sun is strong, so white predominates: white wicker chairs, polar-bear-white carpets in the spacious bedrooms, greeny-white orchids growing in big pots, and white louvered window shutters.

The spa forms part of the hotel. Here the wealthy and fashionable take the waters or follow the latest health and beauty treatments in its immaculate orchid-filled rooms. They may eat Michel Guérard's Cuisine Minceur, for its exquisite dishes, so pleasing to the eye and so delicious, are also slimming. The alternative is his Cuisine Gourmande, artistic perfection accorded four Gault-Millau red toques, and still very light on cream and butter.

Early days in his father's butcher's shop near Rouen, apprenticeship to a pastry chef, and running a celebrated restaurant in the suburbs of Paris have all helped to give Michel Guérard's cooking the polished

perfection it has today. A meal here is an experience to treasure. Following delicious canapés, six exquisite courses began with fresh foie gras. A delicate confection of asparagus tips, truffles, and wild mushrooms was followed by half a lobster, smoked and then lightly cooked on a special charcoal grill installed in one corner of the spectacular kitchens, which gleam with antique-style brass-trimmed ovens. Meltingly tender duck, tiny vegetables – a little disconcertingly presented in the duck's webbed foot – seasonal fruit sorbets, and delicious hand-made chocolates with perfect coffee concluded the meal. Wine was from Michel Guérard's own vineyards, and the chef himself in immaculate whites appeared to greet his fortunate guests.

The hotel is ranged around a sunny courtyard (opposite). The fame of Michel Guérard's cooking is world-wide: above is a selection of his sorbets. Overleaf: left, a view of the spa and one of the bedrooms; right, the gardens and the billiard room.

LES PRÉS D'EUGÉNIE, 40320 Eugénie-les-Bains. Tel. 58 51 19 01. Reservations: 58 51 19 50. **Owners** Michel and Christine Guérard. **Director** George Mootz. **Closed** 15 Dec.–1 Mar. **Rooms** 28 double, 7 suites, all with bathroom (with wall shower), direct-dial phone, TV. **Facilities** Drawing room, bar, restaurant, billiard room, 2 elevators, extensive gardens, pool, 2 tennis courts, spa with beauty and health treatments, helicopter landing. **Terms** Deluxe. **Credit cards** Amex, Diners, Visa. **Getting there** From Paris, A10 to Bordeaux, A630/A63 s, N134 round Mont de Marzan, N124 to Grenade, D11 to Eugénie-les-Bains. 731 km. **Of local interest** Medieval buildings dating from the English occupation of Gascony after the marriage of Eleanor of Aquitaine and Henry Plantagenet are scattered throughout the area; Roquefort. **Whole day expeditions** Romanesque churches of old pilgrim route from Paris to Santiago de Compostela; seasonal music festivals; motor racing; flower-filled city of Pau; Pyrenees mountain villages; Lourdes; Biarritz and beaches, Spain. **Lunching out** Domaine de Bassibé, Aire-s-l'Adour; La Ripa Alta, Plaisance.

25 L'Oustau de Baumanière

A breathtaking setting

The setting is extraordinary: a landscape of white rocks, fantastically sculpted by wind and weather into twisted shapes and caverns, among the pine and almond trees in the perfumed, sleepy air of Provence. A ruined castle stands on a high crag, and at its foot lies the beautifully restored medieval village of Les Baux and the Oustau de Baumanière.

Raymond Thuilier, grandchild and great-grandchild of innkeeping bakers (his widowed mother cooked for a station buffet) studied law and rose to be head of a large insurance company. But after World War II, approaching fifty, he decided to return to his family tradition. He repaired the Oustau, an ancient Provençal farmhouse in the Alpilles, in the Rhône delta between Avignon and Arles, and set about cooking with a zest and creativity that won him first one, then two, and finally three Michelin stars. The Queen of England and other heads of state as well as the wealthy and the famous have come to this enchanting place: the clientele remains as select today. M. Thuilier himself, turning from one art form to another, began to spend his spare moments painting, and his grandson, Jean-André Charial, took over much of the daily organization, following a demanding training in top French kitchens.

At night, the scene is unforgettable: floodlit castle and village above, the white rock formations all about gleaming in the moonlight, the swimming pool a brilliant blue, its terrace with white chairs and tablecloths patterned in blue flowers set against the stone walls and candle-lit windows of the restaurant. The restaurant, in the heart of the Oustau, is a long barrel-vaulted cellar supported on massive pillars, with a smaller sitting room next door. Behind are wine cellars with a treasure-trove of many tens of thousands of bottles of fabulous wine. The choice of dishes is impressive, the service polished, and the flowered tablecloths are dressed with silver candle-sticks and fine crystal. Frogs' legs and quail eggs in a cress salad, sole with grapes and a hint of ginger, tenderly pink roast duck, served with pears, local cheese, a frozen nougat with a fresh strawberry coulis: all were excellent.

The bedrooms, scattered round the main house, are all different from one another. Some are complete little medieval houses, with stone floors and canopied beds, open hearths and tapestried walls; others are snugly buried in the thick walls, close carpeted and with dainty furniture. Some are reached by steep flights of stone steps, others by car. There are further simpler rooms at the Cabro d'Or, the village inn owned by the Oustau, which has its own pool and tennis courts, and puts less strain on the purse for those who wish to invest significantly in the meals and wines.

Thanks to Raymond Thuilier, and now to his grandson Jean-André Charial, life has returned to this village, lost in the wild countryside of the Alpilles, the ancient domain of the Lords of Baux.

Towering outcrops of rock loom over the hotel (opposite); the famous restaurant is in a converted wine-cellar. Overleaf: the terrace makes an idyllic setting for summer meals.

L'OUSTAU DE BAUMANIÈRE, 13520 Les Baux de Provence. **Tel.** 90 54 33 07. **Telex** 420 203F. **Owners** Raymond Thuilier and Jean-André Charial. **Closed** Late Jan.–early Mar. and all day Wed. and Thurs. lunch in winter. **Rooms** 25 (incl. 11 suites) (22 more rooms at Cabro d'Or), all with bathroom (incl. wall shower), direct-dial phone, TV. **Facilities** Sitting room, restaurant, garden, terraces, pool, tennis, riding, helicopter landing. **Restrictions** None. **Credit cards** Access, Amex, Visa. **Getting there** From Paris, A6/A7 past Avignon, exit on D99 W dir. Nîmes, turn L for Les Baux. 716 km. **Terms** Deluxe. **Of local interest** Arles (Roman theater and amphitheater); Avignon (papal palace, ramparts, museum etc); Nîmes (Roman amphitheater); Pont-du-Gard (Roman aqueduct); Uzès (restored medieval town). **Whole day expeditions** Camargue (wildfowl and white horses), Saintes Maries-de-la-Mer, Aigues Mortes; Aix-en-Provence; Senanque and Silvacane (12th-century abbeys). **Lunching out** Brunel, Avignon; Les Frênes, Montfavet (see p. 83).

A gentleman's residence

Seat of the Popes in the 13th and 14th centuries for a hundred years, Avignon is a place of massive buttressed walls and tall towers, battlements and ramparts, palaces and churches, that spill over the Rhône to Villeneuve-les-Avignons on the other bank. The famous bridge of the nursery song survived only until the 17th century, when much of it was washed away, leaving just four arches still standing. The ancient Greeks colonized Marseille, and the Romans have left amphitheaters in Nîmes and Arles, but Avignon is a medieval city, guarding the waterway of the Rhône as it flows down to the delta and the marshes of the Camargue, where flocks of wildfowl and pink flamingos live, and where the famous white horses and black bulls are raised.

Set in a quiet back street of Montfavet, a village on the outskirts of Avignon, the shady gardens of Les Frênes are cool and inviting in the hot sunshine, filled with flowers and birdsong, dotted with the ash trees from which the house takes its name. The large pool, surrounded by statuary, is a good place to relax after a busy day sightseeing. This pleasing mansion, with shutters and balustraded terrace, has a variety of bedrooms, and it is well to specify one's tastes when booking. Those by the pool have either pastel decor and twenties-style furniture with angular modern lines, or traditional provincial rustic pieces. In the house, some rooms are quietly understated and restful, others exuberantly period: one at the top of the house is furnished entirely with ornate pink, Louis XV Chinese-inspired pieces.

The large bedroom in which I slept was a masterpiece of exuberance, which I loved, though anyone who arrived envisaging the plain lines of a modern bedroom might find it somewhat overpowering. The brown and white speckled marble fireplace had ornate firedogs below a vast mirror with gilded frame and a gilded clock and pair of decorated vases on the mantelpiece. The flocked wallpaper had a complex design of blue and gold, the ceiling was moulded into flowers and foliage, and a chandelier glittered with crystal droplets. Elaborate carving on the massive wooden wardrobe matched that on the head and foot of the enormous bed, over which hung a carved and gilded trophy of violins, arrows, ribbons, and laurel leaves. Ornate brass lamps entwined with cupids stood beside the bed, and bedcover and table and window draperies were in shades of blue. Even the bathroom shelf had ornamented brass brackets. But modern comforts were not forgotten: a powerful shower, a minibar, color television with video, and windows screened against insects.

The starred Michelin menu specializes in fresh Provençal produce, is well-balanced and includes local dishes; breakfasts are sumptuous, and the owners, Jacques and Eliane Biancone and their son, spare no efforts to ensure the greater comfort of their guests.

Sunshine gilds the statues by the pool in this charming mansion (opposite); decor in the bedrooms ranges from ornate grandeur to art deco chic (above).

HOSTELLERIE LES FRÊNES, Avenue Vertes Rives, Avignon-Montfavet 84140. **Tel.** 90 31 17 93. **Telex** 431 164F. **Owners** Jacques and Eliane Biancone. **Closed** End Oct.–early Mar. **Rooms** 20 (incl. 4 suites), all with bathroom (incl. wall shower), radio, direct-dial phone, TV with hotel video channel, minibar. **Facilities** Sitting room, restaurant, elevator, gardens, pool, tennis, sauna, games room, free lock-up garage, golf at private club (with tuition) by arrangement. **Restrictions** None. **Terms** Expensive.

Credit cards All major cards. **Getting there** From Paris, A6/A7, exit Avignon Sud in direction of Avignon. At traffic circle, take turning to Montfavet Valence and at third traffic light turn R; hotel is on L after approx. 200 yards. 680 km. **Of local interest** Avignon old town. **Whole day expeditions** Senanque and Silvacane abbeys; Pont-du-Gard; Nîmes; Arles; Alpilles. **Lunching out** Oustau de Baumanière, Les Baux (see p. 79); Auberge de Noves, Noves (see p. 85).

27 Auberge de Noves

Provençal pleasures

An old manor house, built in 1812, set about with hillside fields and orchards, the Auberge de Noves was in ruins when bought in 1955 by Monsieur Lalleman. Restored with love and taste, it has kept its own strongly Provençal personality when other hotels have succumbed to international glitz. On the shaded terraces outside you can sit and sip your breakfast coffee, or eat your evening meal looking out at the pine trees and misty blue distances that inspired Cézanne and Van Gogh. The bedrooms are furnished, as Monsieur Lalleman says, "like my grandfather's house," with local wooden furniture and Provençal designs: bold flowers, strong colors, vivid reds, sharp yellows, lush purples. Bathrooms, however, are tiled and modern.

I ate inside, sheltering from the Mistral, the cloud-dispelling wind of the south, and had an excellent meal admiring the view. Each table was laid with a cream damask cloth, brown and yellow local pottery plates and table lamp, well-polished silver, and a small *santon*, one of the local carved figures in traditional regional costume. The restaurant had a wide wooden fireplace, interesting local antiques, enormous fresh flower arrangements, and was filled with French families quietly appreciating the food and the wine from the lavishly stocked cellars. Appetizers placed on the table included olives stuffed with goat's cheese, and freshly baked cheese straws topped with slivers of almonds. I was delighted to find a regional menu offered, and chose a delicious mousseline of fresh trout with fennel, followed by duck breast wrapped in pastry and surrounded by a subtle red wine sauce. Vegetables served on a side plate were excellent. After a modest browse among the generous selection on the cheeseboard, I enjoyed *paillard de pommes reinettes*, a succulent form of apple pie served with a fresh raspberry coulis. I was then urged to sample something from the complimentary cold trolley loaded with elegant silver jars, and succumbed to a mouthful of caramel icecream and a dab of orange sorbet. With the coffee arrived a large dish of very tiny exquisite petits fours.

The Michelin judges are stern: they have awarded the restaurant at the Auberge de Noves from nought to three stars at different times, the current rating being one. Monsieur Lalleman said with a wry smile and philosophical shrug of the shoulders that he felt the cooking had always been much the same standard. Certainly on my first visit I found everything to be faultless.

The destiny of the Auberge lies with Monsieur Lalleman's son, who will eventually take over its management. One wonders whether he will wish to follow the fashion of the day, or whether, given a growing interest in traditional recipes and fast-vanishing local traditions, he will allow it to stay as it is: a friendly, relaxing Provençal inn, with excellent food and its own endearing personality.

The magnificent food can be enjoyed in the beautiful dining room or on the terrace with its splendid views. A corner of one of the delightfully simple bedrooms is shown above.

AUBERGE DE NOVES, 13550 Noves. **Tel.** 90 94 19 21. **Telex** 431 312F. **Fax** 90 94 47 76. **Owners** The Lalleman family. **Closed** Early Jan.–end Feb.; Wed. lunch. **Rooms** 23, all with bathroom (incl. shower cubicle), minibar, direct-dial phone, TV; most have airconditioning. **Facilities** Sitting room, restaurant, terrace, elevator, gardens, swimming-pool, tennis. **Restrictions** None. **Terms** Expensive. **Credit cards** Access, Amex, Visa. **Getting there** From Paris, A6/A7 exit Avignon Sud. N7 s, D28 w dir. Châteaurenard. Hotel is 2 km from Avignon Sud. (NB direct flights available from Paris to Avignon; courtesy car will collect by arrangement.) 691 km. **Of local interest** Avignon (papal palace, ramparts, museums, Villeneuve, etc.); Arles (Roman amphitheater); Nîmes (Roman amphitheater); Les Baux and Alpilles. **Whole day expeditions** Pont-du-Gard (Roman aqueduct); Uzès (restored medieval town); Camargue (wildfowl, including flamingoes, and white horses); Saintes Maries-de-la-Mer; Aigues Mortes; Aix-en-Provence; Senanque and Silvacane abbeys; beaches. **Lunching out** Oustau de Baumanière, Les Baux (see p. 79); Les Frênes, Montfavet (see p. 83).

International glamor

When I arrived at the Moulin de Mougins I learned that Roger Vergé was not present. The great and famous chefs of France are sometimes reproached for their peripatetic lifestyle, and I was interested to see if, with the master away, standards would sag. In lesser establishments I know unfortunately from experience that they sometimes do. I am happy to report that I found everything to be superb.

The setting is delightful: an ancient mill, built in the 1500s to crush olives for their oil and still working until the 1960s, when it was bought by Roger Vergé. You turn off the main autoroute along the Côte d'Azur, opposite Cannes. As you go up the hill, you turn off sharply to the left, down a steep drive, to find the Moulin. The old mill is charming and has massive stone walls. The entrance is creeper-covered and there is a view into a leafy garden with huge earthenware pots of flowers on one side, and a river, rosebeds, reeds, and a hillside rising steeply on the other. There is a snug sitting area with a welcoming fire and huge cascading flower-arrangements, inner low-beamed rooms with prints on the walls, tapestried dining chairs and stiffly starched table-cloths. The outside terraces have rattan chairs and white awnings spread above them like sails.

At dinner there was a small square glass vase of vivid yellow nasturtiums on my table. Delicious hot canapés accompanied my aperitif while I studied a menu which looked both interesting and appetising. The food arrived under domed food-covers, made of pretty pink and white pottery rather than the more usual silver. Breton lobster was served in a delicate saffron and orange sauce, sea-perch and scallops in tarragon butter. A mouthful of grapefruit and vermouth water-ice was followed by duck with wood-mushrooms, in a red Margaux wine sauce with apples, and a selection of cheeses from Savoy. I finished with the Moulin's own nougat glacée, accompanied by a coulis of red fruits. Coffee was brought on a small brass tray, together with a plate of perfect *gourmandises*.

The bedrooms are small but decorated with taste and charm, antique furniture and flowery fabrics, and some have terraces. It is essential to book very well in advance. Gourmets come from all over the world to eat here, and many would also like to stay, or attend cookery courses at the Amandier. This was created in 1977, eight years after the Moulin, and is also a restaurant, simpler but in the same style. Like the Moulin, it is in Mougins and is under Roger Vergé's direction.

Those searching for trophies to take home need look no further than the boutique at the Moulin, which is well supplied with tempting bottles and jars.

Roger Vergé, a three-star Michelin chef, travels all over the world to cook – to East Africa, to the Carribean, to Walt Disney's Epcot. But he has a superb back-up team headed by his son-in-law, Serge Chollet, as well as polite, expert, and welcoming restaurant staff. The presence of Roger Vergé, silver haired and with magnificent moustache, must add enjoyment to a visit, but in his absence the splendid quality of his cuisine is maintained.

Roger Vergé and his chefs provide spectacular gourmet pleasures (above); this ancient watermill has been skilfully converted into an outstanding hotel (opposite).

MOULIN DE MOUGINS, quartier Notre Dame de Vie, 06250 Mougins. **Tel.** 93 75 78 24. **Telex** 970 732F. **Owner** Roger Vergé. **Closed** End Jan.–20 Mar., 15 July–30 Aug. all day Mon., Thurs. lunch. **Rooms** 5 (incl. 2 suites), all with bathroom (incl. wall shower), direct-dial phone, color TV. **Facilities** Restaurant, terrace, bar/sitting room, boutique, gardens, helicopter landing. **Restrictions** None. **Terms** Deluxe. **Credit cards** Amex, Diners, Visa. **Getting there** From Paris, A6/A7/A8 to Cannes; exit dir. Grasse N, hotel on L before Mougins. 950 km. **Of local interest** Flower fields and perfume factories, Grasse; Cannes. **Whole day expeditions** Iles de Lerins; Cap d'Antibes; Nice; Vence. **Lunching out** L'Amandier, Mougins; Château du Domaine Saint-Martin, Vence (see p. 89).

29 Château du Domaine Saint-Martin Vence Côte d'Azur

A crusader's stronghold

When exhausted by the demands of a busy life, this is where many of the famous come to relax, away from the heat of the coast, among the ancient olive groves and pine trees, in the clear cool air of the hills above Nice and Vence. The Château du Domaine Saint-Martin owns a series of little *bastides*, small separate Provençal stone houses, built on the hillside above the château, private and peaceful, yet fully served by the hotel – even, if wished, with all meals. There are also apartments among the trees by the heart-shaped pool. The bedrooms in the château itself are mainly spacious, with an elegant, cool, almost monastic air, and look down over terraces to the broad sweep of the coastline and the sea beyond.

The commanding site, once fortified by the Romans, and visited in 350 by St Martin, bishop of Tours, was given to the Knights Templar, on their return from the Crusades in 1115, by the Count of Provence, on condition that they till the land and protect the people. There is a romantic legend that the treasure of the Knights lies buried undiscovered in the grounds of the château. Of the crusader castle only the gateway, drawbridge and one tower remain, blended skilfully in the mid-1930s into the structure of a luxurious private mansion for Monsieur Genève, father of the present owners.

Well-clipped tall hedges enclose the courtyard and creeper-draped entrance, which leads to a circular hall, a long gallery with arched windows, and a small salon. The huge drawing room beyond is furnished with fine antiques and Persian carpets. The large terrace restaurant, partly glassed-in, has spectacular views, which at night change to a galaxy of twinkling lights. Meals are served with style, and the food is formally presented in silver or copper dishes, rather than pre-arranged on a plate. Fresh eggs, herbs and olive oil are from the estate, vegetables are grown locally, and the menu, which includes Provençal specialities, is Michelin-starred.

My bedroom, leading off a wide, red-tiled terrace, was in the main house. Plain white walls, a tan carpet, buttercup-yellow bedcover, a superb antique desk, and some pleasant prints made up a restful, simple decor. There was a round table on which a delicious breakfast was formally set out on a cloth in the morning, and at night the bed was turned down, a small linen mat placed beside it, and the shutters closed. The bathroom was spacious and tiled, with a good shower.

Nearby is the picturesque walled town of St-Paul-de-Vence, and the beaches of the Côte d'Azur are fifteen minutes away by road.

The château is managed with quiet, self-effacing efficiency by Mademoiselle Andrée Brunet and a well-trained staff, invisible until required. Guests feel they are staying in their own luxurious private château, and can relax in its peaceful beauty.

The remains of the Crusader castle are glimpsed through its original drawbridge (opposite). The interiors and grounds (above and overleaf) embody 20th-century luxury.

CHÂTEAU DU DOMAINE SAINT-MARTIN, route de Coursegoules, 06140 Vence. **Tel.** 93 58 02 02. **Telex** 470 282F. **Owners** The Genève family. **Manager** Mlle Andrée Brunet. **Closed** Open all year. **Rooms** 25 (incl. 10 suites), all with bathroom (some with wall shower), direct-dial phone, TV, 21 with minibar. **Facilities** Drawing room, salon, gallery, restaurant, terraces, extensive gardens and grounds, swimming pool, tennis, some lock-up garages, helicopter landing. **Restrictions** None. **Terms** Deluxe. **Credit cards** All major cards. **Getting there** From Paris, A6/A7/A8, Cagnes/Vence exit, through Vence dir. Coursegoules, D2 N, hotel on L. 1000 km. **Of local interest** Vence and St-Paul-de-Vence, both medieval towns with notable modern art galleries; Matisse Chapel; Colombe d'Or (inn with art collection); Cagnes (art gallery, castle, Renoir's house); Biot (Léger Museum); beaches. **Whole day expeditions** St-Jean-Cap-Ferrat (Ephrussi Rothschild Foundation); Nice; Monaco; Eze-Village; Italy. **Lunching out** Le Cagnard, Cagnes-s-mer; Chantecler, Nice; La Reserve, Beaulieu-s-Mer; Chèvre d'Or, Eze-Village (see p. 93).